Flourishing
IN UNIVERSITY AND BEYOND

All the arts we practice are apprenticeship. The big art is our life.
M.C. Richards

John A. Dwyer and Thomas R. Klassen

Library and Archives Canada Cataloguing in Publication

York University Bookstore
4700 Keele Street
Toronto ON M3J 1P3

Dwyer, John, 1948-
Flourishing in university and beyond / John A. Dwyer & Thomas R. Klassen.

ISBN 1-55014-444-8

Previously published 2003 under title: A practical guide to getting a great job after university, by Thomas R. Klassen and John A. Dwyer.

1. College students--Vocational guidance. 2. College graduates--Employment.
3. Success. I. Klassen, Thomas R. (Thomas Richard), 1957- II. Klassen, Thomas R. (Thomas Richard), 1957- Practical guide to getting a great job after university. III. Title.

HF5381.D98 2005   650.14   C2005-904204-4

Printed and bound by York University Printing Services
Cover and Book design by Kathleen Munro

Dedicated to

Dawn Bradley

by John A. Dwyer

and

Sue Han

by Thomas R. Klassen

PREFACE

We wrote this book to answer many of the questions that university students have about how to succeed in their courses and in their post-graduation careers. All of the concerns and questions addressed in this book came from students we have taught at Ryerson University, Trent University, the University of British Columbia and especially York University. At York University, we have particularly benefited from teaching the Foundation courses in the Division of Social Science.

The book, as with any manuscript, is the result of efforts by many. Michael Jackel and Steve Glassman at the York University Bookstore and Printing Services respectively have provided the necessary resources. Our colleagues in the Faculty of Arts encouraged us to write a work that integrates university studies and life skills, learning objectives that are too often separated. Michael Legris, also at the Bookstore, has been a steadfast advocate of this book, at its previous edition, which was titled *A Practical Guide to Getting a Great Job After University.*

Jill Andrew, Virginia Galt and Melissa Hughes provided us with useful comments and feedback on the previous edition of the book, which allowed us to undertake this expanded version. As important were the remarks we received from dozens of students who found the first edition helpful. A number of teachers and advisors at several universities also contributed their observations on the first edition.

For this edition, we have added chapters four, five and six, as well as revised the other chapters to take into account the feedback. We continue to seek to break down the barriers between the university experience and post-graduation careers. We continue to believe that the skills for academic and employment success are similar, and that these can be learned. Most important, we believe that success in school and work will naturally flow when individual motivation and understanding work together.

We especially thank Dawn Bradley for her invaluable editorial assistance.

TABLE OF
CONTENTS

CHAPTER ONE

HOW TO USE UNIVERSITY TO PREPARE FOR A GREAT JOB

The best time is always the present time, because it alone offers the opportunity for action.

George Vanier

INTRODUCTION

Obtaining a university education is more expensive than ever, and more competitive. Unlike in the past, completing a degree is not a guarantee of a job, much less a good job. The labour market is more cutthroat with fewer good jobs. Canadians, especially new graduates, are competing for jobs not only with each other but often also with people in and from other countries.

Although many students know that university is important to get a great job, sometimes it is difficult to see the relationship between university and work. Many courses seem irrelevant or overly abstract and your professors may appear to have little understanding or appreciation of the *real* world. Sure, Shakespeare, Marx and Plato are important to them, but what about to your future employers? Many of your bosses and older colleagues, particularly in smaller companies, may not have even attended university and probably don't appreciate the hard work that is involved in the academic process. As a result, it is easy to become cynical or depressed about doing the necessary tasks - the assignments, tests and exams - that are required to complete a degree.

Most people take at least three or four years to complete their under-graduate degree. By the time you finish, you will have paid a great deal of money for that little piece of paper. One university course costs in excess of $1,500 after you have paid for books and related expenses. In total, your B.A. or B.Sc. will cost you at least $28,000 and possibly more if you need to re-take courses or change programs. Some programs, such as business and computer science, will set you back an additional several thousand dollars in tuition. If you attend a university away from your home, the total cost for a B.A. or B.Sc. could be $60,000.

As if all that wasn't bad enough, it gets worse. Ahead of you, and perhaps blocking your way, there is a generation of employed Canadians who didn't need a university degree to get a decent job. When you complete university you will join the 20% of other Canadian adults who have successfully completed a university education. You will have worked hard, and made many sacrifices — perhaps supported by your family — to join this elite group. But these days a cap and gown is no guarantee that you will find a promising career.

To fully enjoy the fruits of your efforts, your degree should be followed by a great job. The good news is that it can and will if you play your cards right. That implies being smart and strategic about how you prepare for the job market and translate the skills you've learned at university into something more marketable!

This is a practical guide to help you, today's university student, learn the skills you need to do well in university courses and today's challenging job market. The guide applies to all university students, many college students and high school students, and their parents'. It is a book that should be read and acted on from the time you begin your university studies. But there is a lot in here that will help those who are about to leave university for the real world.

This is also a book that will help you *flourish* as a student, a professional and as a person. The concept of flourishing is as old as ancient Greece. It involves maximizing both your self-development and your contribution to society. Ultimately, it is all about the happiness that comes when you live a thoughtful, balanced and self-directed life. Don't be misled by these high sounding words, however. There is nothing impractical about flourishing.

Many individuals in today's world don't flourish either at university or in the workplace because they obsess about getting a great job with a big paycheck. They respond uncritically to social values and pressures (including parental pressure). Society constantly bombards you with messages about getting into one of the elite professions or taking specific courses and programs that have a *pay off*.

Your university experience and life will only be diminished if you give into this kind of tunnel vision. University education can and does lead to financially rewarding and fulfilling jobs. But universities don't and shouldn't function simply as employment mills.

That task would be hopeless in any case. No one can predict with perfect accuracy what the job market will be like in the three to four years it takes to complete a degree. It makes more sense to enjoy your university experience rather than constantly worrying about your future. At the same time, it is good common sense to try to broker your university experience into something that helps you succeed in your working life after your degree. You will be able to flourish much better in university, work and your life if you pay attention to this dynamic relationship.

Not understanding exactly how school relates to work, or how to get the kind of job you want, means that you're not fully taking advantage of your years at university to prepare yourself for the labour market. You don't have to be totally consumed with getting a job; in fact, we'll show you how an obsession with gainful employment will probably backfire on you. But at the very least you should be giving the relationship between school and work adequate consideration.

The more you understand the relationship between your university experience and the real world, the more prepared and the less stressed you will be about your future. And you'll have much more fun at university as well!

WHAT'S UNIVERSITY ALL ABOUT?

"I don't think we're in Kansas anymore, Toto." The classic line from *The Wizard of Oz* sums up the experience of many students who are new to university. The standards are higher and the competition for good grades is tougher. And, to top it all off, the social and cultural transition from high school to university makes everything more difficult.

University is all about preparation for the rest of your life, not just your job. You'll discover things you never imagined that interest you. You'll learn to think and communicate. You'll make new friends and you could even meet your life partner. You will definitely learn lots about love, life and academe, but much of it will not seem applicable to your job and career after graduation.

University is a time of many things: learning, meeting new people, making decisions, new relationships, maybe moving out from your parents' home, traveling, dealing with money problems, working part-time and sometimes even full-time, and more. However, the years in university are also valuable periods that could - and should - be spent preparing for life in the workforce after university.

But, as we explain in this book, there is nothing better than university as the training ground for the career of your dreams! The bonus is that you can enjoy your years at university as much as you like, while still making sure that you're ready to land the job of your dreams after graduation. Does this sound too good to be true? Read on.

WHAT TO EXPECT AFTER GRADUATION

One of the greatest uncertainties about being in university is what will happen after graduation. Will I find a career? Will my job be one that I like? Could I end up unemployed? Will my job pay enough? Might I have to move somewhere else to find work I like? Will I get stuck in a rat race? These are critical questions. Fortunately, many can be answered right now.

When you graduate, you will enter a professional workplace that is very different from the one that your parents experienced. Not so very long ago, a university degree was the ticket to a good and presumably permanent position. However, today's organizations are seeking a very different kind of professional - a flexible problem solver who: 1) is good at multi-tasking; 2) adapts well to change; and 3) is a team player. People change jobs and the jobs themselves are changing constantly.

Your parents will not always understand the pressure that you are under, since they didn't experience the *same kind* of pressure. They may want you to get a stable position and become self-sufficient as expeditiously as possible. But the modern world is anything but stable; in order to become truly self-sufficient, you need to be much more proactive and flexible than they needed to be.

Your career trajectory will be tougher than many of your parents. That doesn't mean it will be worse and it certainly doesn't mean that it will be less interesting. It does mean, however, that you can't be passive about anything. You need to be strategic, creative and opportunistic.

Permanence is a thing of the past. Today's public and private sector employers are not looking for someone who will stay with the organization all of his or her life. They expect professional people to seek new opportunities every five years or so, and they realize that a significant percentage of present employees will be moving on, looking for better challenges and remuneration. In many modern professions, staying too long in one place can even be interpreted negatively — it can imply that the individual lacks ambition! That's the reality of the new world of work that you will be entering.

As a student, it is perfectly normal to hope for a stable and permanent position as the reward for several years of hard work without a livable income. Just be aware that the modern professional marketplace is extremely fluid and change is the norm rather than the exception. The skills that you develop as a university student will help you adjust to inevitable changes in your life.

All the prognosticators agree that the professionals of the future will need to be lifelong learners. They will continually update or develop new skills as these are needed. Learning is being transformed from a stage in the life cycle into a continuous process. Individuals will need to take far greater responsibility for seeking out the information and educational opportunities that they need to keep abreast of their field or career trajectory. Those who are passive or reactive will be left behind.

Given the importance of learning in your future professional life, it only makes sense to learn right while at university. Many university courses provide an ideal training ground in the kind of critical and communication skills that will allow you to sift what you need from the plethora of information in the new knowledge-based economy.

These are exactly the kind of skills that will make you adaptable. Your university years offer a unique time when you can develop those skills without the kind of pressure that comes from holding down a full-time job.

Now, some of what we are going to teach you about *learning* undoubtedly will seem a bit abstract at first. But stick with us and we'll show you how to demonstrate in very practical terms skills that may at first seem subjective or ambiguous — the identical skills that modern employers are looking for.

As a future professional you will need to develop four sets of skills to succeed in your career:

> · excellent communication skills (reading, writing, speaking, listening);
>
> · a demonstrated capacity for value-added (i.e. critical and creative) thinking;

- the ability to learn and solve problems, rather than simply following instructions;

- teamwork, including social skills (ethics, positive attitude, responsibility);

- a willingness to adapt to changing circumstances and to transfer knowledge to new situations.

The more of these skills you can acquire, the better prepared you will be to contribute to your profession and to fulfill your career goals. Guess what? These skills (no more and no less) are the key to success in university as well.

MONEY

Usually, but not always, a great job comes with a good salary. The majority, but not all university graduates, will end up in well paying jobs. You want to be on the winning side of this equation.

Money doesn't guarantee happiness, but it sure as hell doesn't hurt either. A good income is probably a necessity since more than half of all graduates begin their first jobs mired in debt. Paying back your loan(s), and having money to travel, buy some of the things you've been deprived of, maybe even get married should be a good incentive to take career preparation and the job search process seriously.

The good news is that two years after graduating with a bachelor's degree you likely will be earning about $40,000.[1] This is the average, of course. That means some graduates will be earning considerably more and others less. The trick is to be in the group that earns more, and, equally important, enjoys what they do!

HOW TO SELECT COURSES

One of the most stressful aspects of attending university is deciding on your major, program or specialization and courses. Sure, you get advice from guidance teachers, university counselors, parents and family, but it is ultimately your decision. And it is a BIG decision. Of course, some choices may not even be feasible because of various requirements and pre-requisites for specific programs of study. But there are still tons of choices that you have to make. Here is the best piece of advice we will give you in this book. Make these choices on your own, not somebody else's terms!

The most sage advice, and the advice you might not get very often, is to trust yourself. Select programs and courses that interest you, without worrying too much *initially* about getting a job after graduation or earning a good salary. Yes, without considering the labour market! This is the most sensible approach because, ultimately, you need to find satisfaction in your courses, just as you will need to obtain satisfaction from your work after graduation.

For example, there is no sense taking accounting courses only to fail them because you have zero interest in accounting. Similarly, a significant number of students take a Bachelor's degree in business because they or their parents believe that it will provide them with a great job. The business curriculum is difficult and inflexible. After four years, some of these students end up detesting business so much that they would rather do anything else with their lives. What a waste of four years!

Wouldn't it be preferable to complete a degree in a subject that you like and that you want to do well in? After that, you can always do an MBA full-time or part-time if you are still interested in the business route. Our point is that you don't have to make yourself miserable; you have choices. They should be *your* choices!

As you will see a little later in this book, the road to a great job has many, many paths. Your path must be the one that is most enticing to you. Don't make the horrendous mistake of associating your future success with how painful the process of getting there is. At this stage, *don't worry, be happy* is a better philosophy.

Here's the good news. Pick the courses that appeal to you. That is the best guarantee that you will do well in them, and doing well (not necessarily getting straight A's) in courses is necessary to get a great job. Being frustrated, unhappy, failing courses you dislike, constantly changing majors or programs, is not a good road to a great job. It is also an unnecessarily expensive and *painful* way of getting an education.

MATURE, RETURNING AND PART-TIME STUDENTS

You may find that for a number of reasons, including getting burned out (almost everyone experiences burnout at some point in their lives; it's no biggie), you decide to study part-time or return to university as a mature student. One of the really neat things about university is that it's always there for you, and that you have choices about how and when to organize your learning.

That's one of the good things about modern life and the need for lifelong learning. If your parents went to university, most people were about the same age. While this was great for dating and party purposes, it excluded lots of people who didn't feel that they belonged in a postsecondary institution. Nowadays, it's not uncommon to find pensioners and seventeen year olds in the same classroom, especially in continuing education programs.

Not everyone can or should study full-time. Part-time programs are available in many fields of study. In some cases, you may be told that you cannot enroll in a program on a part-time basis. This should not necessarily discourage you, as there may be creative ways to accomplish what you want to do.

Here's our second most valuable piece of advice. Never simply accept something that a bureaucrat or administrator tells you at face value. Do a little bit of exploring and try to see the people who make the actual decisions. Rules almost always allow for exceptions and much of your present and future success depends on how proactive you are. There is a saying – "the squeaky wheel gets the grease" – if you get what we mean.

Studying part-time can be a good strategy for a period of time during your university studies, maybe just a summer or maybe for a year or for your entire university education. For example, many full-time students regard the summer as a period to make some money or recover from the academic grind, only to find themselves bored stiff or working for minimum wage or both. Wouldn't it make better sense to do a course in something you are interested in and decrease your workload the following year?

Whoever invented the idea that university education only takes place between September and April? Probably the same misguided souls who think you are too old to go to university once you reach twenty-five or get married. That's very old-fashioned thinking and completely out of touch with modern life.

Seriously considering part-time education also reinforces one of the most important truths about the new world of work, which totally endorses lifelong, episodic and strategic learning. The days when postsecondary education was confined to a few years at university or college are rapidly vanishing, to say the least. Don't get hung up on an outdated model.

If you cannot attend a post-secondary institution right out of high school as a full time student, that's okay. In some cases, for professional programs, such as law and teaching, having several years of *not* being in school is seen as an advantage.

To tell the truth, professors (including the ones who wrote this book) usually like students who have taken a break from school for a while. These students tend to be more motivated, have better listening skills, and have already learned the lesson that they must take courses that appeal to them in order to succeed.

Returning students face particular issues in relating school to their experience in the workforce, and vice-versa. Sometimes they become too instrumental, that is, so concerned about how their education relates to the job market that they forget the joy of learning. In the last chapter we cover some matters related to returning to school after having been in the workforce for a while.

WHAT JOB RELATED SKILLS CAN I LEARN IN MY COURSES?

Nearly all the skills you will learn and use in your courses are the identical ones you will need for an interesting, challenging and well paying job. Surprised?

Doing oral presentations, working in groups, meeting deadlines, overcoming challenges, looking at problems from different perspectives, concisely summarizing information, identifying links and patterns, locating and sifting sources of information, explaining events that have happened and projecting what may happen in the future, writing well and with some analytical depth, dealing with peers and people in positions of authority are almost certainly involved to some extent in your ideal job. These are the skills that you can, and should, develop at university.

Consider any professional occupation or any senior position in the private or public sector. People in these positions spend hours each day communicating with others: convincing them of new ideas and proposals, obtaining and understanding information, explaining matters in person or via writing. Considerable time and effort is also spent looking at events and circumstances in a critical and creative manner to solve problems and make improvements: Why did we have a loss this quarter? How could we develop a stronger and timelier strategy? Why did some of my students fail? Why were the ethics of our organization breached? How does what happened yesterday relate to what happened last month? Finally, anyone who wants to be a professional must have the ability to work with others: colleagues, clients, supervisors, subordinates, customers and other stakeholders.

One of the authors of this book worked for a year as Acting Placement Director for a prestigious business school where students were recruited by some leading Canadian and global corporations. What all of these well-known companies were looking for – even more than high grades – was the ability to solve problems creatively, to communicate effectively, and to work as part of a team.

When looking at resumes or interviewing candidates, the recruiters for blue chip companies look for evidence that these *universal* skills have been learned. They expertly and rather ruthlessly sift out those who simply have good memories, think *inside the box*, or lack those all important people skills.

Universities are very good at encouraging the development of the skills outlined above. But, while there is no doubt that higher education is one of the best investments a person can make, it is *not a* guarantee of a good and fulfilling position. You need to use your years in university to acquire, and practice, the all important four sets of skills:

- communicating,

- problem solving,

- teamwork,

- adaptability.

The amazing thing is that by doing so you will succeed wonderfully in your courses, and also find the time to enjoy all the other benefits that a university education provides.

In the following chapters we will give you hints and advice on how to acquire – in your courses – the skills that guarantee success at school and work. In chapter two, we look in more depth at the general skills that you can, and must, acquire at university to ensure your success as a professional. In chapter three, we will show you how to use the essays, reports, and exams you write for your courses to prepare yourself for your first job and career. Chapter four shows you how to acquire the critical skills that are the key to success in university. Chapters five and six consider the problem solving skills required to deal with university and the workplace and, more generally, life situations. Thereafter, we'll get into the mechanics of the post-university job search.

There is one point that needs to be made before proceeding. The skills that work in university and the labour market may be virtually identical. They do, however, need to be adapted or contextualized appropriately. While the skill set may be the same, the time frame, expectations and environment are different.

Nobody ever claimed that university was the *real world*. However, the path from university to the real world is straightforward and exciting if you know what you are doing.

NOTES

[1] Allen, Mary and Chantal Vaillancourt. 2004. *Class of 2000: Profile of postsecondary graduates and student debt.* Statistics Canada Research Paper (81-595-MIE2004016). Ottawa.

See also:
Allen, M S. Harris and G. Butlin. 2003. *Finding their way: A profile of young Canadian graduates.* Statistics Canada Research Paper (81-595-MIE20003003). Ottawa.

CHAPTER TWO

SKILLS FOR SUCCESS AT SCHOOL AND WORK: BECOMING A PROFESSIONAL

There is only one thing more painful than learning from experience and that is not learning from experience.

Archibald McLeish

INTRODUCTION

There are a number of skills that all professionals need; the primary one is the ability to communicate well. After all, what lawyer, social worker, teacher, business executive, manager, entrepreneur, journalist or any other professional can achieve success in his or her career without first-rate communication skills? Ideally, both oral and written skills are required. But, without strong evidence of at least one of these skills, or competency in both, you can probably kiss your career prospects goodbye.

In this chapter we show you how some of the most neglected, and disliked, aspects of your university courses will be invaluable in your post-university activities. Our experience convinces us that the suggestions we provide below on oral presentations, group work, becoming a proactive professional, taking notes and getting yourself organized will not only make your life easier in university, but also after you start your post-graduation job. Let's begin with oral presentations.

ORAL PRESENTATIONS

For many students, giving an oral presentation in a class or tutorial is among the least appealing aspects of the university experience. The symptoms of presentation flu include sweaty palms, stomach butterflies, and total paralysis. It is stressful and seems time consuming, plus you never quite know what to expect. Yet, oral presentations in courses are among the most job-related activities that university life has to offer.

We prefer to use a broad definition of oral presentations. At the formal end of the scale, you may have to stand up in front of a class and present on a topic of your instructor's or your own choosing. But such presentations differ in intensity rather than in kind from many more casual interactions in the classroom.

The same is true in the world of work. Unless your employer locks you away in the basement, you will give many oral presentations when you begin full time work. You will be responsible for explaining something, communicating your ideas to others, encouraging those you interact with, and so forth. Your audiences for your presentations will include clients, customers, colleagues, investors, supervisors, maybe the general public, and so forth.

If you plan to become a manager or owner, a substantial part of your day will be taken up with preparing, delivering and reacting to presentations of one kind or another. Even if you do not deliver many presentations in your first job, you will likely be responsible for preparing these for your supervisor. In any case, those who hire you and those you work with will be less than impressed if you have poor presentation skills.

Many a promising career has been sabotaged by the inability to communicate well. In fact, many upwardly mobile executives spend a lot of their own or their employer's money to improve in the art of communication. So why not learn to do it now, when the stakes are not nearly as high?

Unless you have good presentations skills you will have great trouble even getting a job. After all, your first oral presentation for your employer will be your interview! Since today's jobs are rarely employment for life, you may have to endure many of these intense ordeals if you want to advance your career or even keep working.

Given how important presentations are in the world of work, why not use the presentations in your courses as practice? If your course requires a formal oral presentation, try to schedule your course presentations early in the term, when there are fewer conflicts with tests and other assignments. Also, learn how to utilize PowerPoint or other computer presentation software in your presentation. Your employer, colleagues and clients will expect that you know how to use such software and associated technologies.

If there are no scheduled oral presentations in your courses, you will still have many opportunities to develop your verbal skills. Asking questions of your professor or tutorial/lab assistant is a type of oral presentation in miniature. Even speaking to instructors during office hours or in other situations is a form of presentation, for which you should prepare if you want to be effective. Speaking in front of your colleagues or with your instructors is stressful, but if you follow the steps below, it will become less so. You might even begin to enjoy it!

Unless absolutely necessary, try not to read your presentation from a script. Do not over-prepare so as to become mechanical in your presentation. Aim to be yourself, which is much easier if you have done the necessary research and preparation that makes you feel that you are an expert. For anyone who has read or understood less than you — even your teacher — you are the expert!

Don't forget our first and best piece of advice to you. All of the above is made so much easier if the topic of your presentation interests you. After all, why speak on something that bores you (and others) to tears. Thus, the key is to take courses (and ultimately be in a career) on subjects that satisfy you.

Even if you are stuck with a bad topic — let's say others take all the good topics — don't settle for mediocrity. It is a very uncreative person who can't find something interesting in even the most unappealing topic. Would you want to hire someone like that?

This leads us to the overwhelming key to success as a presenter. Enthusiasm. Nothing is more contagious, effective, and compelling than enthusiasm. The best teachers and the best presenters are the ones who convey personal enthusiasm. When combined with knowledge and a little practice, the effect can be awesome.

All this preparing may seem like a lot of time and effort. But it is not really, partly because the more you prepare and rehearse for one presentation, the easier the next one will be. You may think that you have little time to prepare for your class presentation, but that's life. The sooner you learn to suck it up the better. You will be expected to spend the required preparation time for presentations when you are working full-time after graduation.

The time and effort invested in presentations in school will pay off handsomely in but a few years. Formal (large audiences) and casual (breakfast and lunch meetings) presentations are a common way of sharing information in today's professional world. Chances are that presentations will dictate much of your daily life as a professional.

You will have far less time to prepare when you are employed. Your employer, as well as your clients and colleagues, will expect you to be able to hit the ground running. Why not take advantage of the time you have to get good at it now?

Think some people are just better at verbal communication than others? The truth is that anyone can improve these skills significantly. One of the authors of this book has a disability that most of you don't have to worry about. He stammers. Nevertheless, he's learned to become a highly effective teacher, lecturer and communicator.

When you are good at something difficult, it becomes satisfying and even pleasurable. Giving presentations is obviously difficult, so giving an effective presentation can be amazing. Just check out the faces of your classmates following a successful presentation if you don't believe us.

The more you practice, the easier it gets. A large portion of the mark of students in management programs is quite logically based on their presentation skills. After a few years, business students treat presentations not only as a routine requirement, but also as an opportunity to impress.

Treat presentations as an opportunity to develop a useful skill, to demonstrate the ability to simplify material, and to really impress your instructors and classmates (and more importantly, yourself). Here are a few tips for formal presentations that you can adapt to your own situation:

· Be proactive. Always think of a presentation as a chance to impress everyone, not just with how hard you have worked, but how clever and original you have been.

· Have a dress rehearsal. Practice makes perfect. Practice in front of the mirror, or your siblings, friends or others. Video or audiotape yourself if you can. Do this whether it is just a question you plan to ask in class tomorrow or a lengthier presentation.

· Appearance is half the battle. Dress well to show everyone how serious you are about the presentation and how much respect you have for your audience.

· Arrive early. Get to the presentation room at least a half an hour before your presentation is to begin. Check all your equipment. Go over your notes. Decide how you are going to greet people.

· Organize all your materials. Have handouts in a place where people can get them on the way in. Make sure that all audio-visual materials are ordered properly (you can order all kinds of audio-visual equipment to be available for you in any classroom at any time).

· Provide a warm welcome. Get your audience on your side right away. Make sure to introduce yourself. Remember that the audience is on your side. They want you to succeed.

· Smile a lot, but don't joke around. One bad joke can kill you.

- Appear confident and composed, even if your stomach is full of butterflies.

- Talk directly to your audience. Never read from notes if you can help it. Have notes available only in case you get stuck.

- Don't try to be too clever. Not only will the audience be confused, but you probably will be too!

- Watch the mannerisms. Everyone has nervous tics. Practice in front of others so that you can identify, eliminate, or transform them into useful gestures.

- Vary the activities. Remember that some listeners have a ten-minute attention span; five minutes if last night was pub night!

- Personalize the presentation and the audio-visual aids so that you look like a real person rather than an automaton.

- Present people with a really clear summary that can be useful as a guide to study for the exam. Your teacher and fellow students will enjoy your presentation that much better if it also saves them some work.

- Always try to have at least one surprise up your sleeve. If you can provide extra value that no one expected, your presentation will be memorable. If the environment is right, bring candies or other goodies to distribute. Be creative in this.

- Finish strong and don't be overly modest. False modesty is for losers. Winners try to leave with a bang.

- Take criticism constructively. No one likes criticism. But if it means that you will do better next time, it's well worth it.

WHY PRESENTATIONS?

You may be thinking that oral presentations are overrated. But consider why your professor and employer choose presentations over other modes of communicating information or ideas.

- Presentations are the most personalized delivery of material. Consider how powerful oral presentations are at convincing and persuading an audience to buy a product or consider an idea.

- Consider as well that about half of all interpersonal communication takes the form of facial expressions and body language.

- People learn better when they see and hear at the same time. A good presentation allows the audience to see and hear the speaker. The appropriate use of slides, overheads or presentation materials helps the audience to internalize and remember the material.

- The printed page cannot easily display the range of rhetorical styles and devices that are available to a good speaker. Speakers, for example, can pause for effect; adjust to feedback; change tone and emphasis; and invite and answer questions.

- A well-prepared and well-delivered presentation demonstrates a real commitment to your audience. By showing that level of respect for the audience, the presenter also earns far greater respect for his or her subject matter than would be possible in any other format.

The six most common mistakes made by presenters

1. Not projecting clearly

The greatest presentation in the world is useless if people can't hear it. Use a microphone if you need to. Better still, practice speaking in different venues in order to ensure that you are heard clearly by everyone in the room. Many presenters speak too quietly and have a tendency to mumble, especially when they are relying on notes.

2. Not making eye contact with the audience

One of the advantages of a presentation is the potential for interactivity and rapport with the audience. These cannot be achieved, however, unless the presenter makes a conscious effort to maintain eye contact with the audience.

3. Way too much information

This is the biggest mistake of inexperienced and insecure presenters. They often make the mistake of trying to do too much. They are more worried about having enough to say than communicating with their audience. A good rule of thumb is that your audience can retain no more than three big ideas illustrated by two or three examples each in a one-hour presentation. More than that and people will begin tuning you out.

4. Running over time

How do you feel about teachers or professors that keep talking after the designated time? There is no better way to sabotage an otherwise good presentation than by running over time. The message that you send to your audience is that your time is more important than their time, which completely defeats the atmosphere of mutual respect that you have been working to develop. If you think that you are going to run out of time, simply leave things out. Trust us, the audience won't notice.

To avoid the unpardonable sin of running over time, try to prepare a talk that will run 10 minutes shorter than your allotted time. That not only ensures that you will finish on time, but also provides you with a few minutes to take questions at the end.

5. Handing out materials during your presentation

Make materials available before or after your presentation. Only hand out materials during a presentation if you are going to go through those materials completely with the audience. The minute that materials are being passed around, people get distracted. Some will begin reading and will no longer be following what you are saying. You will need to work extra hard to regain their attention. It's much smarter not to lose it in the first place.

6. Inappropriate use of audio-visual aids

Don't be seduced by technology! The keys to a successful presentation rarely depend upon whiz band audio-visual effects, and these enhancements can be a huge distraction if not used properly or if they don't work well. We've all attended presentations that started late because of technical hitches, and most of us have even had to cool our heels in the middle of some presentations while technical adjustments were made. If you do use audio-visual aids, make certain that they are:

- employed appropriately and in context;

- used to enhance, rather than distract from, what the speaker is saying;

- tested by you before the presentation;

- simple and easy to see or hear.

Questions and answers

For many presenters the most stress-inducing part of a presentation is when the audience asks questions, especially your professor (or your boss). But, remember you are in charge. The presenter controls all the dynamics of the presentation and structures the framework for questions and answers.

Set the ground rules at the start of your presentation to favour the skills that you have. If you don't wish to answer questions until the end, say so at the beginning. On the other hand, if you want to maintain an atmosphere of interactivity you can ask for the audience to raise questions as your presentation proceeds.

Encouraging the audience to ask questions about anything that seems unclear is a good way of inviting them into a relationship with you. It is the invitation to ask questions, rather than the questions themselves that is most important.

Make the invitation for questions genuine. Don't just say "any questions?" and sit down. Give them an invitation to interact. Say something like "I hope that you have some questions for me" or "Is there anything that you would like me to clarify or that you would like to explore further?"

Maintain eye contact with the audience. Smile. Wait. Twenty seconds can seem like twenty minutes when you are waiting for people to ask questions. They need time to get into questioning mode. Give them the time.

Whenever you get a question, repeat it for the audience. Not only does this affirm the importance that you attach to the question and gratifies the questioner, but it also invites everyone in the room to share in the question.

Rephrase negative questions in a positive way. Negative questions are sometimes referred to as interjections or interventions and usually mean that someone is trying to show how intelligent they are at your expense. The very worst thing that you can do is to try to shut down the questioner, since it negates your accessibility. Simply highlight the positive.

Never bluff or lose your composure. You are not expected to know everything. If you don't know, say so. But don't stop there. Say that you will be happy to get that information for anyone who is interested and leaves his or her name and address at the end of the presentation. If you are experienced in retaking control of the discussion, you can even throw the question out to the audience to see if anyone there has an answer. But don't try this unless you know how to get the attention back to you.

Politely end unproductive questions or discussions. You are in charge. The audience expects you to gently prevent someone else from rambling on or to establish closure on discussions that are going down dead ends. Remind people why you are doing this by saying something like, "Can you complete your question so that we can entertain as many questions as possible in the next few minutes?" "I'm sure that there are lots of other issues that people want to raise; let's move on."

Turn weak questions into good questions. If someone asks you a weak question, you have an opportunity to demonstrate skill and really win over your audience. Good presenters are experts at finding a grain of brilliance in a bad question and turning it to their advantage. Rarely will the questioner challenge your interpretation of the question, since it has now been transformed into something very flattering to them. The most intelligent people in the audience will appreciate how you've handled an awkward situation and protected the individual's dignity at the same time. It's a win-win situation for everyone.

Always thank the audience for asking questions. Tell them that you found them to be a good audience. They will be much more inclined to think of you as a good presenter if they believe that you consider them to be a good audience.

Hopefully, you will now view oral presentations not so much as a chore, but as something valuable, interesting and even fun. We now want to move on to show the benefits of another activity that is often disliked by students, but is almost as vital for your success in the workplace.

GROUP WORK

When you were in high school, you probably engaged in at least some group work. In the hands of good teachers, group work can be fun and exhilarating. But some of you may have felt that you did most of the work while others got to share all of the credit. Given the democratic and coddling nature of the high school environment, you may still believe group work is a waste of your precious time.

Don't let past experiences cloud your judgment about the value of group work. In the modern world of work, people rarely operate in isolation. The success of companies and organizations today is based on effective collaboration. And, unlike in high school, if you don't contribute to the success of the group, your reputation will suffer and you won't last long.

Today's business community and employer marketplace is big on team-work and collaboration. Teams, therefore, give almost all presentations in business schools and in many other professional university programs. What's fascinating about group presentations is the way that individuals build on their own particular areas of expertise to come up with something much better than they would ever have been able to achieve on their own.

Despite these advantages, group projects do have their own frustrations. Almost always with group projects there are disagreements about how to proceed; things take a long time to work out; and not everyone works equally hard. This is especially true in university classes, where many of the worst habits of high school often continue.

However, you must learn to overcome your frustration. You can be guaranteed that in your future job you will work primarily within groups. Writing an essay (or other document) on your own and submitting it to one person for review is quite rare in the workplace. Most activities that take place at work are group based. In fact, being able to work well in a group setting will get you jobs, while having few group working skills will cost you jobs and promotions.

The reason why group work is crucial is that nearly all activities at any workplace involve complex undertakings that are beyond the skills of any one person. It's not enough to do something well, but you have to do it at least as well as your competition. This means that you will be part of one or more teams in any jobs you have. Even if you are self-employed you will need to work collaboratively with clients, suppliers and many others.

Use your years in university to hone your skills at working with others. Try to be in different types of groups: with males and females, with older and younger students, etc. Try different roles in the group; sometimes be a leader and sometimes a follower.

Observe how groups work. Watch how others behave and react. Think about how the group could have worked differently. See what impact gender, ethnic background and other factors make in how the group works. Pay attention to the way the final product benefits from this diversity of experiences and viewpoints.

Collaborative presentations and projects pose distinct challenges. Here are some additional tips that you can adapt to any interaction that you have with groups of people:

- Always engage in a group brainstorming session before deciding on a strategy. Don't let one person dictate the strategy. Everyone needs to have ownership of the project.

- Make sure that everyone's role in the presentation or project is clear. But also make sure that everyone understands that this does not absolve him or her of responsibility for the project as a whole.

- Be prepared to eject someone from the group if they are dragging their feet. This may be difficult if you are a student, but the group can approach an instructor (and later on your boss!) for help in dealing with people who don't pull their weight.

- Act as a team during the presentation or project. If you do not have a role to play at a particular time, your role is either: 1) showing interest in and support for what your colleagues are doing, or 2) reflecting group solidarity with clients or audiences. Always be prepared to help your colleagues out if they run into difficulty with any problems.

- Don't showboat. Within group activities there is a tendency for men to assume leadership roles and dominate. This has a negative impact on the group presentation or project as a whole.

- Achieve closure. Celebrate the completion of a project with your colleagues. However impermanent, you became an effective team and you want to show one another gratitude and respect.

As with oral presentations, we hope you might now see group work as an interesting and valuable activity. Look for opportunities to develop these skills.

You may notice that many of your professors are graying. They were educated at a time when individual achievement was valued more highly than collaboration. You might need to encourage them a bit with respect to group work. You will be surprised how many professors will respond positively if you ask whether you can work on an essay, report or presentation with one or more persons. Your enthusiasm will increase their enthusiasm.

The effectiveness of collaboration is something that every progressive employer understands. So, if you want to work for a "with it" company or organization, be prepared to let go of the temptation to fly solo.

The *real magic* of group work is that an effective whole is always more than the sum of its parts. What you can achieve working with others collaboratively is a quantum leap over what you can achieve alone. The destination is well worth any frustration along the way, and the time spent is well spent.

PRACTICE BEING A PROACTIVE PROFESSIONAL

Proactive individuals, sometimes referred to as *self-starters*, are in high demand in today's workplace. The problem is that too many university students are passive and want to be spoon-fed by their instructors. To the extent that you fall into this category, you will not be ready for the real world.

University courses, in some ways, are not that different from work you will likely be engaged in after graduation. At work your manager, or client, will give you vague instructions (just like your professors and TAs) and expect you to figure things out for yourself. If you want a job where you always get clear, specific and detailed instructions, then it will probably not be the job of your dreams, and will certainly not be the work of a professional.

A telling characteristic of "Mc" jobs is that you don't have to think or to be a self-starter. That's why they pay so badly. If you want a good job, let go of the need to have someone always spell things out for you. Take the initiative yourself.

Aim to demonstrate the same type of professionalism at school that you plan to exhibit in the workforce. Be on time with assignments and classes. Read the syllabus carefully. Do your reading before class so that you can benefit from the instructor's interpretation. Chances are that if you treat your classes casually, you will treat your future job casually as well.

That's the real reason why employers are interested in your grades. Good grades themselves are less important than the fact that they probably reflect a person who is conscientious, dedicated and proactive about the education that they are receiving. An A grade implies being well prepared and going beyond what is expected.

Try to figure things out on your own, in a creative manner, rather than running to your TA or professor with every little question. Your boss, clients and colleagues will certainly not appreciate being bothered too often with relatively unimportant questions or requests for reassurance.

Asking for extensions the day an assignment is due may be acceptable in some courses, but will certainly limit your career in whatever job you have after graduation. Having a breakdown in front of your professor due to stress, lack of sleep or poor diet the day before the final exam may get you sympathy. A similar event in front of your boss or client could cost you a promotion, if not your job.

A piece of helpful advice is to avoid asking your professor questions regarding your grades. Feel free to ask about how you might better understand material or improve your performance. After all, the grades are just a reflection of your comprehension and knowledge. In the same manner, your boss (or clients) will react quite poorly to discussions about your pay or how pleased they are with your work, but will be far more interested in discussing the content of the work you have done.

There will be times when you will need something from a professor or TA. Again, approach this situation like a professional – prepare your evidence or question, rehearse, try to analyze the situation. Professors are professionals and TAs are professionals in training. They have many duties to perform in addition to teaching and a perfect right to object to anyone wasting their time.

You may believe that school and work are so different that in school you can be late with assignments, do your work the night before, cram for exams, misplace your books, miss classes, be disorganized, etc. while as soon as you graduate you will become a different person. In a few rare cases this is true, but more likely the way you are during years in university (and the many years of education before that) is a good predictor of what you will be like after graduation. Certainly potential employers have this view, based on many years of experience hiring many university graduates.

Of course, in some important aspects, the classroom is not like the workplace. You have much greater freedom to speak your mind in the classroom than in the workplace. The option to explore issues of personal interest is much greater than most workplaces will ever allow. You can choose not to attend or participate in the classroom with few or no sanctions at all, other than not learning much (after all, you are paying for your university education). Nevertheless, the degree of professionalism that you exhibit in your university activities remains the single best indicator of your performance after graduation.

GENERAL PROFESSIONAL SKILLS

There are other valuable skills that can also be learned at university. It is true that many of these skills can also be learned in other ways, such as from travelling or part-time work. The advantage of learning or strengthening these skills while in the university environment is that you are in a place designed specifically to facilitate learning.

For example, if you live in Toronto, you probably have some appreciation for cultural diversity. But tolerance for cultural diversity is taken much more seriously at university because it reflects breadth of mind and an appreciation for knowledge from a variety of sources. While, university is not the only place to learn about other cultures, most of your teachers will be willing to help you explore these cultural differences. And it sure is a lot easier to learn about others when they are your peers engaged in a safe laboratory designed to promote learning.

Information about other cultures is invaluable in any profession that hopes to succeed in our global economy. Did you know that among Asians, the family name of "Park" is found only among Koreans, and that 25% of all Koreans have this as their family name? So, when you're in your great job, and you meet a client or customer with that name, you'll be a step ahead.

Deep knowledge of other cultures can be very useful. North American organizations can learn a lot from their Japanese counterparts. Japanese corporations are successful partly because they focus on group dynamics as much as individual achievement and because they have a longer-term perspective than our shareholder democracies, with their emphasis on short-term profits.

The university is a place where you are encouraged to systematically explore connections such as those between culture and business. It would be much more difficult, and haphazard, to learn such things on the job. And you probably don't want to ask a new client to explain to you about his culture and family.

In fact, since it is almost guaranteed that you will have clients, customers, colleagues and bosses from other cultures, why not get a step ahead at university? Do you have students in your classes from other cultures and other parts of the world? Why not learn from them? Many professors and experienced students can tell you that students learn at least as much from one another as from their teachers or formal assignments. But the real benefits of a university education are multiplied when formal and informal learning are integrated in a systematic way.

So why not consider being systematic about it? Learn a few phrases from different languages. Learn the appropriate way to greet people (bow, shake hands, one kiss on the cheek or two kisses, or...). Learn about different kinds of people from different backgrounds. Explore other cultures (and perspectives) more deeply.

Don't ever presume that your ethnic community or socio-economic group has all the answers. A more broad-based and in-depth knowledge will make you a better professional in whatever field you enter, from teaching, to science, to business.

An important fact to consider is that many of your classmates in university may ultimately become your clients, colleagues or customers. Consider that senior executives often appoint their university roommates and friends to senior positions. Managers looking for new employees often consult with the people who are working under them. Informal networking and word of mouth are much more important than formal job applications. Who you know may not be as important as what you know. But knowing how to make someone part of your network is crucial. More on networking later on.

Some general skills, while not learned in classrooms, dovetail nicely with university education. The university provides many encouragements and opportunities for people who want to learn computer skills. University labs offer mini-courses or workshops that people outside have to pay handsomely for.

Don't be like an ostrich that hides its head in the sand. Try to keep abreast of technological changes. Using a basic word processing program is no longer an advantage in getting a job. Many employers want individuals who can, at the very least, use spreadsheets, graphic and display software, and Web based tools. If you don't get to learn these as part of your courses, take advantage of the many free workshops on campus, some through the library, and others through campus writing centers that will help you develop these skills.

Finally, a university, particularly a large university, is also a place of work and opportunity. York University, for example, offers you an amazing variety of jobs that can give you valuable experience — some volunteer, but many paid. There exist numerous work-study positions; many professors hire students part time to conduct research, interview groups, and to help run computer labs. In addition, there are dozens, if not hundreds of clubs, sports teams, associations, radio stations, theatre groups, etc.

Many corporations look at a student's resume for evidence of involvement in clubs or athletics. Why will such activities help you get a great job after graduation? Not only do they provide evidence of administrative ability if you hold a significant position or organize activities. But many potential employers are impressed by someone who is able to combine academics with extracurricular involvement; it demonstrates balance, commitment, a willingness to work hard and teamwork.

And let's not forget the obvious, joining a campus or residence group or organization that holds some interest for you will bring you much pleasure and satisfaction. We'll also discuss the networking potential later on.

We trust that you are beginning to get our message. The university is an ideal environment for developing job related skills. Even if your courses don't offer you many opportunities for group work and oral presentations, you can discover these opportunities in other ways on the university campus. Have you begun to realize some of the ways you can make opportunities for yourself?

At this point, you may be thinking that university sure sounds like a great deal of work: classes and all that goes with them, extra workshops on using spreadsheets, and some type of sport or volunteer activity. And it is, if you're serious about that great job. The good news though, is that if are taking courses that you like, and engaged in activities that you enjoy, it will not seem like work at all. It will be fun, as will your future career.

Using numbers

"The time has come, the Walrus said, to speak of other things." Not all of our advice to you is going to sound like fun. Here comes the hard part.

Increasingly, employers need workers who are proficient with numbers. The word they use is that employees should be numerate. More and more, to be a professional means to be able to manipulate and understand quantitative information. More generally, all citizens need a basic understanding of numbers to make informed decisions about investments, loans and banking, and to make sense of the world.

Some of your courses will give you the opportunity to do this, especially courses with some lab work. Some programs of study provide fewer opportunities, but there is always the opportunity to strengthen your comfort level in dealing with numbers.

Typically many social science and humanities students avoid enrolling in courses that seem like they might involve many numbers. This decision is reasonable since quantitative courses (such as statistics and research methods) are demanding and intimidating.

The good news is that such courses are actually hard to fail (almost all students who persevere to the end will pass) and do give you useful skills in the labour force, and other parts of your life. Being able to tell a potential employer during an interview that you have quantitative or research skills will almost always work in your favour.

Another benefit to learning to use numbers is that you do not always have to enroll in a course to improve your skills. Consider learning to use Excel or a similar spreadsheet program; tutorials are often offered free on campus. Or get a friend or classmate to help you to use the software. People just love to show how *numerate* they are!

Using spreadsheet software or even more advanced programs such as SPSS (Statistical Package for the Social Sciences) is not as painful as supposed by even the most mathematically challenged person. The key for many people is to have a specific problem or task. Try to plot your grades. Can you do that? Can you quickly calculate an average using Excel or similar software? Can you plot how much money you will need to invest?

Many term papers and assignments provide opportunities for you to include a helpful table or chart. Look at your textbooks to see how the authors have included charts and tables to quickly illustrate a point, rather than having to write additional paragraphs. Consider using the same strategy. You wouldn't believe how much it will impress your professor, especially if he or she is not particularly *numerate*.

There is such a mystique about numbers that any level of proficiency has a payoff. Learning these skills can be rewarding (dare we say fun?).

A graph, chart or table often increases the grade of an essay or assignment. Without a doubt, the ability to create a simple chart, graph or spreadsheet at times is what differentiates those job candidates offered an employment position from those rejected. You may be certain, that at the very least, many of your bosses, colleagues and clients will expect you to not be afraid of numbers.

Being somewhat numerate may have the biggest payoff in your future career. It is no accident that many of the CEOs and senior managers of large corporations were once Chartered Accountants. You don't need that level of numerical understanding, but your career will be much rougher if you are innumerate.

TAKING NOTES

You may think that taking notes in classes, and from textbooks, is unique to university. In fact, quite the opposite! Taking good notes is something that is integral to just about any professional occupation that you can name.

For example, social workers, police officers, bankers, health care professionals and lawyers must take very detailed notes concerning clients and events. These notes may become critical pieces of evidence in courts of law, often years after they have been taken. Teachers keep notes on the performance of students, which are later summarized in the form of report cards. Journalists and other writers depend on their skills in taking notes. Financial advisors make notes of the preferences and investment advice of their clients, and must be able to quickly recall this information.

For any important meeting in business and government notes will be taken. For the first few years in the labour force, you may well be asked to prepare such minutes of various meetings. One of the authors began his administrative career taking notes at meetings for one of the vice-presidents at York University.

You can be guaranteed that many times during your career you will be asked to "Attend tomorrow's meeting for me and take some notes so I know what happened" and "Read over this report and write me some summary notes." Being able to do such tasks well will get you noticed and rewarded. Doing these tasks poorly, will only get you noticed.

Finally, the office of any professional will contain drawers and drawers of notes taken at professional development courses, observations on the performance of subordinates, remarks on work to be done, various letters and related documents, and commentary on-going projects and activities such as status reports.

The keys to good notes in the professional world, and at university, are exactly the same – i.e. clarity, conciseness and precision. But, notes for school are easier to write because you will be the only reader, while in the workforce you are often writing notes for others to use.

Good notes:

- summarize complex materials succinctly (your boss does not want a transcript of what occurred, rather only a summary);

- organize information in a meaningful way, i.e. from the general to the specific (the meeting you are summarizing may have been chaotic and unfocussed, but your notes of it should be the opposite);

- subsume and subordinate facts and concepts within themes or big ideas;

- highlight the key ideas and elucidate their significance;

- reflect active listening and intellectual dialogue;

- incorporate the insights from different sources (the speaker, readings, past events);

- pinpoint the concepts, issues and problems that require further exploration.

Some of the telltale signs of ineffective note taking, both in university and outside it, are:

- furiously trying to write everything down (there is never any excuse for this because notes are a summary);

- lack of eye contact with the speaker (continue to be engaged with him or her even as you take notes);

- the absence of any questions or issues that need further clarification (if at all possible, ask questions of the speaker(s) to help clarify matters);

- notes that are either disjointed or organized in point form (no one will find these of any help).

Some of the techniques that you can use to develop your skill as a note taker in university include:

- always read the materials that relate to the lecture beforehand;

- leave spaces in your notes to add new ideas later;

- develop your own shorthand to remind you of important connections or questions (i.e. =, ?, N.B.); N.B. is short for the Latin injunction Nota Bene or note well!

- re-read your notes while they are still fresh and make any connections or embellishments that you could not develop during the lecture;

- follow up on any questions that you posed in your notes, either by consulting the readings, your colleagues, or your teacher;

- summarize all your notes on a particular course unit or section on a regular basis;

- compare your notes with the notes of other students in your study group.

The authors have lots of experience teaching university students in large lectures. We can tell you with some authority that a major difference between the students who do well in our courses and those who struggle is their ability to take good notes.

If you don't learn to take good notes in your university courses, be assured that you will find it much more painful and career limiting to have to learn this skill later on.

GETTING YOURSELF ORGANIZED

One of the biggest initial difficulties in tackling tasks at school or work is to be motivated. This, again, reinforces a central concept in this book — that you must select courses and jobs that appeal to you. However, even once you have done so, it can still be difficult to sit down and do the work that needs to be done.

Sometimes we all have a tendency to procrastinate, to get distracted, or to twiddle our thumbs instead of learning. If you think it was easy for us to write this book just because we are professors and interested in the material, think again!

Below are some suggestions that have helped us and will help you get going during those times when you would rather not have to work. These apply equally to school or to the job.

Set yourself goals and sub-goals

Just as you need reasons and goals to get fit or learn a sport, you need to motivate yourself to start the project, whether it is studying for a test, writing a paper or something else. Your overarching goals can be as abstract as becoming a skillful speaker, making a contribution to society, meeting the reasonable expectations of your parents or others.

Your sub-goals should be specific enough to provide you with the rewards that will keep you motivated. Many university students use their career as a goal and good grades as a sub-goal. There's nothing wrong with that, just as long as you realize that good grades also need to be divided into many sub-goals too.

In order to get good grades, you might need to: 1) carefully study the materials; 2) do all the necessary and recommended assignments; 3) attend all the lectures and take good notes; 4) work in study groups with other students; 5) be proactive by doing that little bit of extra research. Reward yourself on a regular basis if you meet these sub-goals. You've earned it!

By breaking down goals carefully into sub-goals, you will avoid the question that paralyzes many students and leads to procrastination. "I've got so much to do, what should I do first?"

Manage your time

Many students do things at the last minute, not because they're lazy, but because it's a quick and dirty method of organizing and motivating themselves. The eighteenth-century writer and inventor of the dictionary, Samuel Johnson, once said that a person could really get focused on the night before he's going to be executed. Some students seem to feel the same way, and some will even try to convince you that they do their best stuff on the night before an assignment is due.

Teachers and experienced students know that is not true, as do successful professionals. Would you want to go to a surgeon who does her work while exhausted, under excessive pressure and drinking cup after cup of coffee?

Some people are better time managers than others. Perhaps their brains are wired differently, or perhaps they absorbed good time management skills from their parents or significant others. But most of us mere mortals need to plan out our time and stick to a schedule. Time is the most precious commodity that a busy university student has; that's why it's so important not to waste it.

Here are some tips to avoid wasting time:

- Force yourself to routinize your time. Try to get up at the same time each morning and go to bed at the same time each night. According to planning experts the establishment of a daily routine is the best way to leverage time spent on task and maximize your accomplishments.

- Create a schedule for your academic term that includes all due dates for assignments and examinations.

- Work backwards from each assignment or examination due date to determine when you should begin working and how many hours you need to invest to be successful in the activity. Most courses, to the frustration of students, are back-end loaded. In other words, most of the work is required late in the term. Minimize this "crunch time" by planning and working far in advance of deadlines.

- Identify priorities. There will always be some subjects or assignments that will be more important than others. Spending a lot of time on an unimportant task is a common mistake made by inexperienced students and professionals. You can identify major priorities by using a different colored ink or type. Always be prepared to adjust priorities as the term evolves.

- Generate weekly and monthly schedules based upon your term schedule (see below). Devote an hour to reviewing these schedules at the end of each week or month, so that you can make any necessary adjustments.

- Aim for steady improvement rather than perfection. This advice is especially important for students who are just beginning to develop a particular skill. There will be some things that you will start out being lousy at. That's life. What's important is getting better over time.

Stay on track

Here are examples of assignment and weekly schedules that students have found helpful for keeping themselves on track. The weekly schedule provides a checklist that allows you to see whether any of the activities need to be rescheduled for the following week. Some students have found it helpful to include rewards like pizza with friends, movie with Sue/Bob, and pub night in their list of activities. Beer is a great motivator, if it comes as a reward for work well done!

ASSIGNMENT PLANNER

This assignment is due on: _____

__Schedule__	__Hours__	__Minutes__	__Target Date__
Background research	_____	_____	_____
Developing a thesis/question	_____	_____	_____
Rough outline	_____	_____	_____
Composition	_____	_____	_____
Documentation	_____	_____	_____
Proofreading	_____	_____	_____
Completed assignment	_____	_____	_____

*By working backwards, you can establish a timetable for completing the assignment. The timetable will become even more effective as you become more familiar with how long it takes on average to complete the various parts of assignments. The safety net gives you a little bit of room, just in case problems arise.

Source: York University Counseling and Development Office

WEEKLY PLANNER

Week of: _____

Activity	Goal	Components	Time Scheduled	Done
Statistics Exam	B+	Review of readings	3 hrs	____
		Review notes	1 hr	____
		Graphs and tables	1.5 hrs	____
		Study group meeting	2 hrs	____
Sociology	B	Read chapters 6 and 7	2.5 hrs	____
		Do chapter questions	1 hr	____
Psychology	A	Attend lab	1.5 hrs	____
		Read chapter 5	1.5 hrs	____
		Q and A session	1 hr	____
History	B	Design Decision Model	3.5 hrs	____

Source: York University Counseling and Development Office

Deal effectively with distractions

The French existentialist philosopher, Jean-Paul Sartre, once wrote "Hell is other people." It certainly may seem that way when you are trying to work and your friends, parents, siblings or other students want to talk to you or get you to do something with them. There are certain things that you can do, such as studying in the library or letting the voice mail take your calls, to keep these interruptions to a minimum. But you will never be able to eliminate them entirely.

Most people don't understand, don't remember, or conveniently forget, how intrusive these interruptions can be. People can be easily offended if you tell them, "Sorry but I'm working on a project. I'll call you later." How you deal with these interruptions can shape your student experience and even your career. Those who learn how to deal firmly but gently with intruders and distractions are usually the people who achieve the most, earn the most respect, and become leaders.

The difference in intelligence between people is very small. The people that we classify as achievers or as brilliant are usually not much different from you or I. They are people who have learned to focus on the problem at hand and to give it their full and complete attention. To do that you need to minimize the distractions.

Here are a few tips on minimizing distractions while keeping your friends:

- Let people know when you are busy and when you will be available.

- Be firm so that people will understand that your academic work is important to you.

- Try to be consistent so that people will know where they stand and will recognize that you are not rejecting them.

- Make a point of following up with these people at times when you are free to engage with them.

- Give people your full attention when you are free to do so. That way they will come to value the *quality* rather than the *quantity* of time that they spend with you.

Make new friends among those who have similar goals and objectives as you, and who appreciate the importance of focused attention. You can even combine social interaction with academic achievement by forming a study group. Some terrific friendships and potential future networks come out of study groups.

One of the reasons for attending university is to meet new people and make new friends. The friendships you make on campus can last a lifetime. It's only when you let your social life interfere too much with your academic life that a problem emerges. Students who learn how to balance their social and academic life usually do well at university and in their future life.

On the other hand, more students drop out of university because they over privilege their social life than for any other reason. The temptation can seem overwhelming, especially when you are released from the constraints imposed by high school, teachers and parents. That's why it is especially important for students who move away from home and parental controls to develop the internal fortitude that goes with performing well at university.

If you don't have these skills well developed by the time you hit the workforce, you will be in trouble. If you are organized, and have the capacity to focus, you already have a good head start on many of your peers.

CHAPTER THREE

PROSPERING IN THE CLASSROOM AND WORKPLACE: EXAMS AND ESSAYS

Experience is that marvelous thing that enables you to recognize a mistake when you make it again.

F. P. Jones

INTRODUCTION

In this chapter we will show you how to perform well on essays, reports, and exams while also using this work to prepare for similar challenges in your career. Most students, quite logically, spend substantial time writing essays and other assignments, such as lab reports, as well as preparing for exams. Why not use that experience as a springboard to workplace success?

This kind of academic work is excellent practice because in your career you will spend considerable time researching, writing and you will be faced with important exams. In fact, the exams in the real world will be of far greater consequence than those you write in university. If you fail a test or exam in school, you may drop your course grade, or in the worst-case scenario fail a course. Failing an exam in the labour force may well cost you a job, or at least opportunities for advancement (and the associated increase in earnings).

Let's begin with exams.

EXAMS

You may think that exams are the least transferable skill that you will learn in university. In other words, you will write few exams at work. However, most professionals have to write many more exams after completing their undergraduate education.

It is not uncommon for job interviews to involve written exams. For instance, for jobs in the public and foreign service, police and firefighting and others, you will need to pass various tests before you will even be considered for an interview.

Even if there is no written component in the application for a professional job, the interview is a test or a kind of exam on what you have learned and how well you can organize and present your thoughts and ideas. If you have not learned to recall important information, respond to unexpected questions, and be analytical, it will be difficult to do well in an interview for any professional position.

Many professionals, including primary and secondary school teachers, must write competency exams every few years. Many other professionals - lawyers, accountants, engineers, physiotherapists and others - need to write qualifying exams, which are often long (sometimes days or weeks) and demanding. Becoming an accountant or an actuary requires many years of arduous exams, characterized by a high failure rate.

Once employed you are likely to take courses that your employer pays for, or that you pay for, for specific credentials, such as to be able to sell securities (stocks and bonds) or insurance, or to learn about new developments in your field of expertise. Usually these courses also involve considerable and lengthy exams.

You may well continue your education by applying for entry into graduate or professional programs, such as an MBA, law school, or a Master's degree. If that is the case, you will need to write exams such as the LSAT (for law school), GMAT (for business school) or GRE (for graduate school).

Finally, many real-life exams and tests will face you each and every day at work. For instance, your boss may ask you to tell her, right now, what the underlying problems are with your latest account. Or, a client may call and ask you to explain why his stock has not performed as you suggested it would two years ago. He's in no mood for bullshit and if you cannot respond to his question, he is taking his business elsewhere. Or, Sabrina's father has come unannounced to your classroom to discuss his daughter's progress. Those are the tests that if you pass, you will be regarded positively by your colleagues and those you work for. If you scramble and flounder, you will most definitely discover that your career will suffer.

Let's face it, exams of any type are anxiety producers. If you don't feel any exam anxiety, pinch yourself, because you're probably dead. Our anxiety about exams is all out of proportion to the significance of the exams themselves, but so what? We are what we feel. Fortunately, we are also what we know. Provided we can control the anxiety to get down to what we know in an examination, we've got a fighting chance of coming out of the process in one piece.

The mere mention of the word exam strikes terror into the hearts of many students. Many years after they have completed their university degrees, graduates still report nightmares about not being able to find the room where an exam is being held. A university instructor only needs to whisper "this might be on the exam" to get the full and riveted attention of a lecture hall of hundreds of students. Even experienced Ph.D. students have been reduced to tears preparing for their comprehensive exams. You would think that by the time someone got that far, they would be a bit more comfortable about this exam thing. No way.

Reducing anxiety

You're never going to eliminate exam or performance related anxiety either at school or at work, but you can reduce it. It makes sense to begin reducing it while at school and to carry that lower anxiety into the workforce.

The most effective ways to reduce exam anxiety in university, in order of importance, are:

- Know your stuff. Understand the material on which you are being examined. In particular, understand the key ideas or themes in a course and the way the facts fit within them.

- Appreciate the positive aspect of stress. Without stress we wouldn't have any incentive to perform to our capacity. Being able to peform under stress is often what separates senior executives from ordinary employees.

- Control excessive stress. Don't let stress paralyze you. Divide your exam preparation into discrete steps so that you don't feel that you are putting all your eggs in one basket. When it all gets too much, get some exercise, watch T.V., or go out for an evening. Learn when to avoid distractions and when to distract yourself productively. Some progressive companies have pool tables in *time out* rooms, so that employees can relax and recharge their batteries.

- Don't cram at the last minute. We know, we know - it worked in high school, right? Well, it won't work at university and certainly not in your career. Bullshit definitely does not baffle brains, whatever its exponents might claim.

- If you simply must cram, make sure that you cram smartly. Just cram in the stuff that stays in your short-term memory, but don't try to learn the key concepts or ideas at the last minute.

- Be aware and stay focused. Here's where the advice of the Zen master and the good student coincide. You can't be stressed out at the same time as you are aware and focused. So it stands to reason that, if you stay aware and focused, you'll control the stress.

· Enjoy the exam experience. Before you tell us to get real, let us ask you a question. When are you most stressed - when you are preparing for an exam or when you sit down and start writing an exam? Chances are that the stress disappears when you concentrate on the task at hand. Be aware. Appreciate the fact that you've now got something better and more urgent to do than worry.

· Put things in perspective. Unless you've been chosen to compete in Mortal Combat, this exam does not qualify as a life or death experience. Believe it or not, many, many people have failed the odd examination and gone on to brilliant careers. One of this book's authors even failed first year university altogether (here's a hint; his initials are J.D.)!

Preparing for a big exam

Not all exams are big exams. It's a waste of time to get anxious or to devote the same preparation for an exam in an easy course that you're acing. For those big scary exams or career making/breaking moments, however, it's good to have a personal strategy.

Here's a strategy that works for some people and that you can customize to your own needs:

· Reduce the pressure on yourself. Concentrate on doing as well as you can do rather than aiming for a specific grade. If you are a perfectionist, put it on the back burner until after the exam.

· Forget about the future. In particular, forget about the impact that this exam might have on your future. Concentrate on the here and now. If you must think about the future, think about how relieved you are going to be when this exam is over.

· Focus. Live and breathe exam preparation rather than the exam itself. Exam preparation is not scary; it's just boring. Prepare to be bored but not scared until the exam is over.

· Complain like crazy. Tell everyone you know that you are preparing for a big exam and that you won't have a social life or a life that's worth living until it's over. The good part about this is that your friends will know better than to bother you. Heck, they won't want to be anywhere near you while you're whining like this. (Judicious whining can work in the workplace too, as long as you do it strategically and with the right people.)

· Organize all your study materials and surroundings. This can be a formal ritual to get you into studying. However, be careful not to let the organization take over from the studying. Some junior executives stay junior executives because they spend more time tidying up their office than at that all-important project they were supposed to have ready by the deadline.

· Build in breaks whether you need them or not. Studying is an open-ended activity. The only thing to stop it is the exam itself. This means that you need to schedule in regular breaks. It's hard to do this in some office jobs, where you are expected to always look busy. But you can learn to take mental breaks without much trouble.

· Identify any major gaps in your knowledge early in the preparation process. Don't wait until the last minute to discover that there are some important issues you do not understand. By then, it will be too late.

· Re-write your notes. Reading over your notes is not the most efficient way to prepare for an exam. By *re-writing* your notes, more of the ideas and the information will stick and you will also make connections that you might not have spotted before.

In the work world, it's always a good idea to go over your presentation or documents close to a meeting to see whether any new ideas emerge that might prove useful. Now is the time to anticipate criticisms and objections, which you can only do if you engage the materials in a fresh and creative way.

Mental clarity and relaxation are often overlooked components for acing exams, as well as for engaging in projects that involve critical and creative thinking. Some keys to relaxing are:

- Don't memorize; make understanding your goal. Memorization is one of the worst ways to organize data. Good exams don't test your capacity to memorize; they examine your capacity to understand material. You may discover that your anxiety level goes down once you no longer have to memorize unrelated data.

- If you have too rigid a script for the challenges that come up in the workplace, you will find yourself inflexible and bedeviled by the details. What you want to take to these situations is a good understanding and an open mind so that you can respond to anything that comes up.

- Get a good night's sleep. On the night before the exam, tell yourself that you've done all that you can. The best thing that you can do for yourself now is to get a good night's sleep so that you will be able to focus all your energy on the exam itself.

Any progressive employer will tell you that mistakes in the workplace happen when employees are suffering from fatigue. But the biggest problem with tiredness is that it saps motivation and cripples creativity.

Workplace fatigue, however, is an important issue that needs to be addressed much more seriously by North American and Asian employers. In countries like Germany and Sweden, employers believe that a substantial vacation and shorter working hours are essential to long-term productivity. The Protestant work ethic in North America and the emphasis on group solidarity in Asia appear to result in greater burnout than is necessary or even advantageous.

The big day

- Make sure you've got what you need, including a couple of pens and pencils.

- Get to the examination room early.

- Pay attention to how nervous other people are. Misery loves company. You are not the only sufferer.

- Feel good because all of this pain will soon be over.

- When you look at the exam, relax and take the time to read over the entire exam.

- Pay attention to the marking scheme. You want to identify the areas that are worth the most and ensure that you don't spend too long on any one area.

- Be strategic. For example, set your sights on finishing the whole exam, rather than achieving perfect marks for part of the exam.

- Focus on the questions. Read them carefully. Read them at least twice. Then read them again. Far too many students concentrate on what they know about the topics on which the questions are based. You won't get the marks if you don't answer the questions.

When translated to the workplace or the boardroom, the advantages of focusing on the task at hand, being prepared, concentrating on what's doable, and being strategic should be obvious.

MULTIPLE-CHOICE EXAM STRATEGIES

There are few multiple-choice exams in the workplace, which to our minds suggests that these are not the best methods for testing a person's understanding or tapping into his or her potential. It is equally doubtful whether much of the real world conforms to the black and white paradigm of multiple-choice scenarios. Unfortunately, there are a lot of multiple-choice exams in professional education as well as in many university subjects. So, whatever their pedagogical (educational) validity, you'd better be prepared for them.

Some undergraduate students actually prefer multiple-choice questions to essay questions. However, the drawback to a multiple-choice exam, from the student's point of view, is that the instructor has complete control over the way that you demonstrate your knowledge. There's usually only one right answer and no shades of gray. Moreover, if ever you are going to find a trick question, it will be on a multiple-choice exam, because trick questions allow the instructor to see how carefully you are reading the questions and making the subtle distinctions.

Studying for a multiple-choice exam is more difficult than studying for any other kind of exam. Multiple-choice exams:

1. require a precise understanding of the material, and not simply a reasonable solution to the problem;

2. mix and match course concepts in ways that are intrinsically confusing;

3. reword concepts in ways that make you have to think about fine distinctions;

4. play with technicalities, analogies and comparisons that take time to decipher (but you usually don't have enough time);

5. force you to think about both the structure and the significance of the question.

Because there are so many possible variables involved in a compressed period of time, it's important to have a very clear strategy for dealing with multiple-choice exams. In particular, it's important to understand why some people get poor marks on these exams. The problems come from: a) reading questions too quickly; b) spending too long trying to figure out one or two questions early on; c) poor exam pacing.

Here's some advice that will help you to eliminate or greatly reduce these problems:

- Do all the easy questions first. Get your brownie points before you do anything else. It will make you feel good, since you will get most of them right. It will prevent you from never getting to some of them because you took too much time on the hard ones.

- Read all the more difficult questions carefully. Circle the key words. See if you know the answer before looking at the alternatives and perhaps becoming confused.

- Then check the alternatives. The alternatives will often trigger an answer. If you know that three answers are incorrect, for example, the remaining answer must be right. Some instructors will present you with questions that have answers that weren't even in the course. They are expecting you to eliminate answers that you know must be false. Pretty sneaky, eh?

- If you don't know the answer, move on. The most natural tendency in the world when you are totally focused is to keep working on a problem. As they say in the fishing industry, there comes a time when it's better to cut bait than to stay stuck.

- Look for patterns and similarities. Obviously, you do this inside the questions when you are trying to discover the best multiple-choice answer. But do this between the questions as well. It's a rare multiple choice where the answer to one question doesn't give you a hint for the answer to another question.

- Take your best guess. Best guesses are not random stabs in the dark. They imply a choice between decreasing levels of probability. Always make certain, however, that you will not have extra marks deducted for errors. In such cases leave the question blank and move on.

- Do not change answers that are guesses. This is a waste of time.

- Watch out for the most typical traps. These include: 1) qualifiers like "always" or "never" that are usually too narrowly defined to be the correct answer; and 2) double negatives in a question that make the right answer a positive.

· Review and review again. If you finish early, it's good advice to keep going over the questions again and again. You are guaranteed to find at least one question that you screwed up because you read it incorrectly. Also, answers to questions will pop into your head as you make associations between different questions.

Although the educational validity of multiple-choice exams is dubious to say the least, they are often used in professional education because they allow teachers to rank students more easily on a bell-curve. If you want to enter a profession or upgrade your professional skills, you will probably run into these sorts of exams periodically. We think that's a shame, but there it is.

WRITTEN EXAM STRATEGIES

Written exams can consist of short answer questions and essay questions. Short answer exams are usually easier to write than essay exams because they tend to: 1) examine factual recall; and 2) they usually can be answered in point form. Essay exams are more difficult because they examine your ability, not only to analyze course materials, but also to synthesize those materials in meaningful ways.

However, essay exams are better at preparing you for your professional career. More often than not, at work you will be asked – often at very short notice – to analyze or explain an event. Why have sales not increased? Why did Sabrina fail? Why was the crime committed? What will happen to our market share? What should be our global strategy?

The advantage of an essay exam is that it puts the ball firmly in your court. You decide how best to address the question in order to show off your understanding of the course materials. As the great English and international soccer player, Stanley Matthews, used to say, he always preferred having the ball, because then he knew exactly what he was going to do with it.

Many of the strategies for a written exam are the same as for a multiple-choice exam. You need to 1) take the time to read the questions carefully; 2) make sure that you divide your time appropriately in terms of the worth of the questions; 3) pace yourself.

In addition to these strategies, you should spend at least 20% of your allocated time generating an outline for each essay. This time is well spent, since it will allow you to compose your essay more quickly and ensure that it will be better organized.

There is yet another reason for taking the time to develop an outline and to include it with your examination answers. If you don't complete your exam within the allotted time, your marker will have visible evidence that you have: 1) mastered the course material; 2) understood the question and had a strategy for answering it; and 3) were only prevented from developing an answer by insufficient time. Many markers will grade a good outline almost as generously as they would an essay response.

In order to do well on essay questions, you need the following:

- a good understanding of the concepts and key ideas of the course, and the relationships between the two;

- strong writing skills, which are discussed later in this chapter;

- to understand and respond to the question!!!

Why the exclamation marks? Consider this awful truth. More students fail essay type exams because they do not pay attention to the precise language and intent of the question than for any other reason.

This message should be imprinted on your brain. If you don't answer the question that is asked, it doesn't matter how much you know, or how much you write down, or how much you understand about the general area to which the topic relates. Unless you have a very kind instructor, you will get a big fat zero. Nothing, nada.

The ability to get to the heart of the question is as important for professionals. Your boss just asked you to tell him or her about last week's meeting that you attended on her behalf. What about last week's meeting does your boss want (and need) to know about? Is it who attended? Or who raised what issues? Or who disagreed with whom? Or why the particular strategy that was developed? Hey, you only have five minutes, or a page, to respond to his or her request "to tell me what happened". If you don't give him or her the appropriate answer, your boss will screw up with their boss, and that is bad news for you.

Or, what is the client really asking about his investments? Is he asking you for a detailed explanation of why money was lost? Or seeking reassurance from you that profits will be made in the future? Or making sure you remember what you told him two years ago? Give him the wrong answer, either in person or in writing, because you did not understand the question correctly, and you'll have one account less.

And what about Sabrina's father? Was he after a detailed question-by-question analysis of Sabrina's last test? Or trying to make sure you're a good teacher? Or something else altogether? You need to be able to respond in any number of ways, but first of all you need to understand the question. Get the question wrong, and your principal will start to wonder about you.

If you misread a multiple-choice question, you only lose a couple of marks. If you misread an essay question on a 3-essay exam, however, the best that you can possibly do is 66%. That's why it's so important to read essay exam questions carefully. The rule of thumb is to spend at least ten minutes breaking down the question and making sure that you've understood it before beginning to write.

To make it even worse, very few essay questions ask you to do really specific things. You won't find many words like list, describe, identify, or summarize in an essay question. And, even if you should be so lucky, chances are that the person who wrote the question still expects you to evidence such skills as: 1) comparing and contrasting; 2) evaluating;

3) ordering in terms of significance; 4) critically analyzing; and 5) synthesizing. Simply the fact that you are dealing with an essay question suggests that these activities are implied.

Unless you have clear instructions otherwise, be prepared to demonstrate your critical skills whenever you confront an essay question. When you run into terms like discuss, analyze, explain, illustrate, outline, or trace, you are being asked to provide a critical analysis (much more on this in the next chapter). The specific meaning of each of these words is less important than the general activity required.

Still, it's useful to think about the distinctions between these terms because they give you hints about what your teacher (or employer) wants from you:

- **trace** suggests that you show the evolution of something from start to finish;

- **outline** means you focus on the main components of something;

- **illustrate** means that you are expected to provide concrete examples to support your argument;

- **explain** means you should give the reasons or the causes of something;

- **discuss** implies weighing the pros and cons of something;

- **criticize** means to evaluate the merit of something in considerable depth;

- **evaluate** - see criticize;

- **interpret** suggests finding a deeper meaning or underlying pattern in something;

- **review** means going over an issue and analyzing it.

But any subtle differences in meaning between these terms pales in significance to the fact that you are expected to provide a critical analysis that breaks down the component parts of an issue to reveal causes, connections and interrelationships. If you want to really excel, you have to demonstrate evidence not only that you can think, but also that you can think creatively and imaginatively.

In the same way, those you will ultimately work with, and for, will want to have on-going evidence that you are critical, creative and imaginative in whatever work you do. They certainly will not pay you a great deal of money to be unoriginal or to repeat common sense knowledge. No, they will want in-depth analysis, concise explanation and plausible options. Exactly the same that your professors asked for!

Essay exams encourage you to play with concepts, build upon the theories of others, and come up with your own interpretations and syntheses. Equally important, they force you to demonstrate these complex skills within a deadline. Lots of people can perform decently given enough time, but the competitive employment marketplace that you will enter is full of deadlines. There's a reason for the word dead in deadlines; if you can't meet or beat deadlines your career will be dead.

Below is a breakdown of three key terms that you will encounter when writing essays, either during exams or term papers. The three terms – compare, argue and assess – are important because they hint at the kind of critical skills that teachers and today's employers are looking for.

Compare	Argue	Assess
To compare means to emphasize the similarities, differences, and linkages between ideas. Your comparison should allow you to illuminate the implications of these ideas and to understand them more deeply.	To argue means to take a position and defend it. An argument is only as strong as the possible alternatives. Don't set up a *straw man*.	To assess means to sift through arguments and evidence using scholarly criteria to build a case. It also implies that you will show how well your case allows you to understand the issues.

Here are the key activities:

Compare	Argue	Assess
Compare - focus on similarities, but take note of differences.	**State** - state precisely the thesis or hypothesis that you intend to prove.	**Review** - explore the range of positions and debates on an issue.
Contrast - focus on differences, but be aware of similarities.	**Prove** - establish the validity of your thesis with logic and evidence.	**Evaluate** - indicate both the strengths and weaknesses.
Connect - show how the ideas are related to one another.	**Debate** - test your argument against other possible arguments.	**Interpret** - simplify complexities so that these issues can be communicated.
Evaluate - if you compare ideas, it is implied that you will evaluate them.	**Justify** - show why your argument is better.	**Judge** - assess the merit, accuracy, or usefulness of different approaches.

Related words

Distinguish	Agree, Disagree, Defend	Interpret, Recommend

Source: York University's Counseling and Development Office (2000)

Work is a continual test!

Can you see how someone with the ability to compare, argue and assess under the pressure of a tight deadline would add value to an organization? If that individual also had the capacity for making accurate judgments, wouldn't they be indispensable? Now add to that an ability to convince others, with a logical argument and relevant data supporting each claim and you've got yourself a worker to die for!

ESSAYS

As we've noted above, being able to answer "why" questions is critical in both school and work. There is no question you will be asked more often in university and your profession. The higher you move in your chosen occupation, the more you will be asked by bosses, colleagues, clients, customers and stakeholders to answer the question *why*. Why did my stocks go down? Why are sales up this quarter? Why are there fewer clients this last quarter? Why is he trying to see me? Why is the project not finished yet? Why is my daughter not doing well in grade two?

Of course, you will be asked other questions too – What stocks should I buy? What should I teach my students? – but these too will also involve having to explain why your answer is the best one.

Thus, the most critical skill to be learned in university is how to explain things. Another way to think of this is that you must learn how to provide others with a convincing *interpretation* that explains a particular development. Not just any old *thing* or *development*, but complex things or developments that are difficult to understand.

At some time during your university career you will be required to write an essay of some type. You are unlikely to write an essay in the workplace and so, quite legitimately, you may feel that the effort required for essays is somewhat wasted, or at least not particularly transferable.

Yet, essays offer the opportunity to sharpen your ability to answer "why?" questions and significantly improve your ability to communicate your findings. Your boss will not ask you for an essay on why sales are down this quarter, but she will want a report that explains why this is the case and recommendations on what can be done to reverse the trend. What is more, your boss will want you to demonstrate the critical and creative thinking that essay writing builds. The topics of critical and creative thinking are explored in more detail in the next chapter and chapter six.

Essay writing teaches you to explain things to others. It doesn't matter whether the subject is: why Byzantine architecture took the particular form it did or why currency and commodity investments are moving between countries at an astonishing rate in the new global community. The interpretive, critical and analytical skills required to explain these developments are fundamentally similar.

Ever wonder how your university professors got to be so smart and so good at understanding and explaining difficult things? They wrote a hell of a lot of essays, case studies or reports. Once they finished their undergraduate degree, they didn't stop writing essays. In order to become professors, they usually had to write an M.A. and a Ph.D. thesis. A thesis is just a really long, original and theoretically informed essay. Once they get to be professors, they have to write articles (shorter essays) and books (longer essays) to keep their jobs and get promoted. You didn't think that all professors did was teach, did you?

You probably don't plan on becoming a professor – at least not just yet — but you can develop the same critical and creative skills for use in your chosen career or profession. Use your essays as ways to practice writing concise, well-grounded and interesting documents. Essays and similar assignments also give you the opportunity to explore the kind of career you want. Use your essays to become an expert in a particular field. Sometimes it can be hard to decide on essay topics, especially if your professor or TA gives you the freedom to select your own question. In this case, why not select a topic that can work to your advantage after graduation?

For instance, why not study the impact of a new trade or human rights international agreement on Canada, and specifically on Canadian companies or other organizations? Or, if there is an issue that is prominent in the media (a discovery, a debate, a tragedy, etc.) why not study an aspect of it, for your humanities, social science or other courses? When you start to look for jobs, even summer or part-time jobs, you can use your knowledge of these developments and changes to show potential employers that you have specialized and current knowledge.

Another example is to study an emerging trend or development. For example, the Canadian population is aging as the baby-boomer generation turns 50. This trend will have many impacts from product development, to health care policy and pensions. If during your university career you write several papers on aspects of the aging population, you will have knowledge that employers will value. The brilliant thing is that just about all organizations will have to deal with the aging population, whether they are auto manufacturers, insurance companies, travel agencies or whatever.

It might be a good time for Nike and Adidas to move some of their assets out of jogging equipment and into golf clubs and apparel. Not many seniors are going to keep on jogging because it's too damned hard on aging joints! Book publishers will have a bonanza when more retired people have time to read. In order to take advantage of that growing market, however, they will need to provide materials of interest and relevance to seniors.

Selecting essay and research topics that have relevance to you and potential employers can be done in any discipline, including philosophy. Scandals in government, fraud in business, crime rates, the rights of individuals and so forth raise some of the key philosophical and ethical questions that are studied by philosophers.

Another beneficial outcome is that once you have completed your research paper you will have a paper that you can take with you to your interview. More on the interview process later on.

As we've noted before, it is crucial to take courses that appeal to you. But why not take the interest thing a step further and pick specific essay topics in those courses that engage you? Then be strategic and look for links between your interests and the kind of things that might appeal to future employers or provide a foundation for a future career. Writing essays, and especially good essays, is work, but work that is fun if related to your interests.

You can build your own unique interests into a smart career strategy. Once you have identified a particular area of interest, you can then explore this through a variety of courses. Over time, you will know more about the subject than most other people. This makes you more of an expert, and ultimately more marketable.

Being objective

It's not enough to be interested in something. To get good at it, you need to approach the subject in a rigorous way. Academic writing, and particularly scientific writing, is the most objective kind of prose. The academic writer has a particular obligation to communicate information that is as precise and correct as possible. Hyperbole, over-dramatic language, and exaggeration are not traits of good academic writing, because they detract from the simple efficiency of the language and prevent clear communication.

Clear communication is absolutely essential in the workplace. Professional and business writing has to be objective to be effective. A report that is dramatic or contains inflated language, or inaccurate information, will result in poor decisions being made. Decisions are (or should be) made solely on facts, evidence, logic and reasonableness. You must be able to write in this manner to succeed in a profession. There is no better way to learn how to write professionally than a university essay, report or case study.

Health care and legal professionals, accountants, social workers, police detectives, nurses, teachers, journalists and all other professionals must be objective and impartial. When they write or speak, they do so only after having carefully weighted and analyzed the facts and considered possible hypotheses to explain those facts. That doesn't mean that you can't have an opinion. It does mean that you need to clearly *articulate* that opinion, *support* it with theories and evidence, and *defend* it against other plausible opinions.

Students often complain that professors are "too picky" or "they should have been able to see what I really meant." These attitudes and the constant whining about grades have no place in academic writing because precision and clarity are exactly what is needed. Stylistic and grammatical mistakes are punished, not necessarily because instructors are sticklers for formal grammar, but because bad writing obscures meaning and impedes effective communication.

Unsupported statements are questioned, not because your professor necessarily disagrees with you, but because they are unscholarly. In the professional world, you will be expected to back up every statement you make. If you have a tendency to make statements off the top of your head or on the basis of emotion/intuition, your employers and colleagues will label you a loose cannon. The problem with loose cannons is that they are inaccurate and continually miss their target. They also get fired or demoted to jobs where they can't do much damage.

A professor may give you some flexibility in being unclear in your argument, or having insufficient evidence, or writing weakly. After all, university is a place to learn, and that means making mistakes. However, you can bet that those paying you, and possibly relying on your expertise in very personal ways, will not cut you any slack. So, the goal is to continually improve and that improvement will be reflected in better marks at university and a better career afterwards.

WRITING FOR THE ACADEMIC READER

Whenever you write, whatever you write, you need to keep your audience in mind. Many students fall into the trap of trying to write for a particular instructor and waste time trying to figure out what will please that particular individual. Some students even go so far as to *pretend* to support ideas or theories that their teacher holds.

This usually is a misguided approach. It may work with one or two instructors, but it's a low percentage strategy. It's far wiser to apply your energy to developing an argument that is academically sound. At least this way you will develop the skills that will make you a better writer at the university level.

Every year, the authors of this book have to give low marks to students who simply try to parrot what they think we want to hear rather than to carefully research and develop a position. It's difficult to respect people who engage in this false form of flattery and don't want to learn for themselves.

The same thing goes for the workplace. Most bosses don't like yes-men or yes-women. Sure, you can write reports and memos to please your boss, but that will not work for long. Once you get a reputation for being this kind of person, your boss won't respect you and your colleagues won't trust you. Your career will be seriously damaged and it may even be difficult to hang on to your self-respect. It is much better to learn to write in a professional manner that suits the environment that you are working in.

When you write an academic essay, all academic readers will expect you to adhere to the following goals:[1]

1. *Completeness and comprehensiveness*

Academic writers must clearly: 1) locate their work within a body of knowledge; 2) demonstrate how their work contributes to that body of knowledge; and 3) proceed from a statement of the problem to its resolution.

A common saying in the workplace is don't re-invent the wheel. Build on the knowledge that is already out there.

2. *Accuracy*

Academic writers must provide information that is accurate. This means that they must check all statements to ensure that they are not obscuring the data or jumping to false conclusions. Accuracy in essay writing demands that students choose their words carefully and expect to be challenged on any statements that cannot be verified.

Your employers and superiors will be particularly harsh with you if you fudge the data, because this could result in incorrect decisions and embarrassing situations.

3. *Impartiality*

Academic writing is impartial. Academics usually state their theoretical frameworks or any biases that they might have up front, so that the readers can judge the organization of the data for themselves. They inform readers of the limitations of their work and tell them about the alternate interpretations that they have rejected. They don't exaggerate the importance of their findings. Most of all, they never sweep inconvenient data under the carpet.

Similarly, your employer or superior relies on impartial information. He or she will usually have many things to take into account in the final decision, including other options, the bottom line, buy-in by management and employees, and the brand image or reputation of the organization. If the decision is based on biased information, it will be doomed from the start.

4. *Order*

This is what beginning writers find most difficult. Academic writing presents materials in a logical order. Difficult or problematic data is introduced carefully so that it does not disrupt the order. Unnecessary information is taken out so that it does not detract from the logical flow. Sections of the essay or document need to be very clear and the transition between sections must demonstrate logical development. Each paragraph should cover a consistent set of ideas

Order and logical development is absolutely crucial in the world of business and government. Usually, documents are headed by an executive summary that condenses the argument but also shows how each point is linked together. If any linkages are loose or missing, the entire report is rejected.

5. *Relevance*

Why do students have such a problem with the order of their material? The first reason is because they haven't organized their research findings clearly. The second reason is that many students are too eager to show their readers how much work they have done and how much they know. Therefore, they try to jam everything into an essay or assignment.

In the past, you may have been rewarded for tenacity and the recall of information. At the university level, we *expect* you to do the work, but we *reward* you for clarity and relevance. That is why you may get a much lower mark than someone who has done far less work than you, and may even know less about the subject than you do.

Employers simply do not tolerate irrelevant or off-track thinking. They are paying you for focusing on the problem at hand, and any digression is not only a waste of their money, but it is a waste of their time.

Here's a business axiom that may help you: don't just work; work smart.

6. *Simplicity*

Academic writing should demonstrate both that you have mastered the material and that you can communicate it effectively. University teachers will challenge you if your words and ideas are not simple and straightforward. The best way to demonstrate that you understand subtle and complex ideas is to put them into simple language.

The authors of this book have written many documents for large public sector organizations in government and university administration. We can tell you that we had to write documents with the utmost simplicity and that we often had to write and re-write documents until they reached that point.

7. *Clarity*

The result of following all of these principles is clarity. Clarity is all about making the complex simple. Clarity is all about distinguishing between logical arguments and emotional appeals. Clarity is all about getting rid of irrelevancies so that you can communicate with greater precision. Clarity is all about focused and elegant language, rather than flowery or convoluted prose. Clarity is all about saying something effectively the first time, rather than repeating it unnecessarily.

If you re-read the above seven points, you will see that each applies to any writing you will do outside of university courses. Who would take you seriously if your proposal, sales presentation, memorandum, legal brief, child custody case report, or whatever was not accurate, or comprehensive, or relevant, or impartial, or concise? Will your professional colleagues, managers and others value your ideas, comments and suggestions if they do not meet the above criteria?

In an environment where time is money, and where your superiors need to make sound decisions based on good information, you will need the skills that come from good essay writing. It is no coincidence that the best writers at university are also the ones that have the most promising careers outside of the ivory tower.

HOW TO ORGANIZE AN ESSAY

Organizing your essay is different from organizing your research. Your research is organized in terms of topics and issues. The topic and its related issues, of course, will always be the critical substance and argument of your essay. The meat of your essay is contained in your research. But good academic essays are also structured according to certain organizational conventions that readers have come to expect.

When you pick up a novel, you expect a certain kind of structure. Poems take various forms depending on whether they are sonnets, elegies, etc. Plays usually have a certain number of acts that vary according to different periods and cultural practices. Similarly, academic essays usually have one or more of the following archetypal structures:

Argumentative

Many scholarly essays and articles are arguments or debates. An argumentative essay must develop a clear thesis or argument that is supported by the evidence. You typically begin by outlining your argument. Then you describe one or more arguments that conflict with your own. After evaluating the merits of all the various arguments, you show why you think your argument or thesis is best.

A critical reader (i.e. your professor) will be looking for evidence that you really appreciate the strengths of the approaches that you disagree with.

Interpretive

An interpretive essay is one that selects and illuminates the evidence within sophisticated concepts or theoretical paradigms. These paradigms are either disciplinary approaches or theoretical models. By applying these approaches or models, you interpret or make sense of the data. Interpretive frameworks are useful to the extent that they can discover patterns within the evidence that go well beyond common sense or intuition. They are one of the most valuable tools that scholars have.

A critical reader will want to see that you understand the theoretical frameworks and are applying them properly. Many students try to use theories without understanding them, with predictable results.

Descriptive

A descriptive essay is one that avoids argumentation and interpretation. The purpose of a descriptive essay is merely to outline a process or convey factual information that will be useful to the reader. Good descriptive essays require the judicious selection of salient facts as well as clear and concise communication.

A critical reader will be asking the question: what's missing from this picture? You can't include everything in a descriptive essay, but you need to make sure that you haven't overlooked points that are significant.

Comparative/exploratory

A comparative essay is one that takes two different approaches to an issue or data set. These can be theoretical frameworks like Freudianism and Marxism or they can be the two sides of a contemporary debate (i.e. abortion, affirmative action). Both approaches are discussed and one is usually preferred over the other.

A critical reader wants to be sure that you have understood the comparative strengths and weaknesses of your approaches, and have a good reason for preferring one to another. The worst thing that you can do is set up a straw man, or a weak interpretation that is easy to tear down.

Incremental

An incremental essay is one that slowly builds from small, seemingly insignificant points, to a powerful conclusion. Each step builds on the one before it to create an impressive edifice.

A critical reader will be looking for missing steps.

Synthetic

A synthetic approach lets you take the most appropriate and relevant elements from the various approaches in order to put together the most powerful argument you can. Good academic arguments are complex and subtle and rarely rely on one single approach.

A critical reader, who appreciates the difficulty in making synthetic arguments, will look to see that you have done a good job of applying the relevant theories and approaches in order to gain insights into the material.

If you re-read the above typology you will see that each essay type has its counter-part in professional settings. At some point in your career you will likely have a report that analyzes two different business strategies and must argue for one, rather than the other. You may have to write a report that tries to explain the failure of a particular project. Or you will write a report that just states the facts as they are.

Good reports or business case studies often contain elements of all of these types. They may begin with a clear and detailed description of the situation or problem. They may build information incrementally and logically to establish a pattern. At some point, they will apply theories and interpretations in order to generate options or alternatives. They may bring theories and approaches together in unique ways to provide more creative solutions.

THE BASIC STRUCTURE OF AN ESSAY

The basic structure of an essay or a professional report is simplicity itself. You have a beginning, middle, and an end. The beginning is the introduction where you introduce your subject. The middle is the body where you develop all the various steps in your argument. The conclusion is the place where you succinctly sum up what you have argued and proven. It may also include any future implications of your findings.

Your essay's introduction

Getting started is half the battle. Don't make it any harder than it already is. You don't need a dynamic opening to get going. You just need to introduce your topic, provide any necessary background, and tell the reader what you intend to prove. This section identifies the major problem, controversy, debate, or question to be examined in the essay.

Although this section is short you need to use it to show the reader the value of what is to follow. The length of the introduction can be a single paragraph or a couple of pages, depending on how complex your topic is. There are no absolute rules.

Many of you will have the concept of a thesis statement drilled into your heads from high school. A lot of guides to writing say that the first sentence of your essay has to be a thesis that spells out exactly what it is you are going to prove. While the intention behind this advice is a good one, the advice itself is nonsense. Many of the greatest essays or most influential reports ever written would fail the thesis test.

What you really want to do is to have a controlling statement that either 1) comes early in your introduction, or 2) you build towards clearly and concisely. The controlling sentence doesn't have to be a thesis statement. It can be the question you want to answer, or a problem you want to explain, or a dilemma you will explore.

A common tendency of students, and writers of professional reports, is to provide the answer to the question, problem or dilemma in the introduction. Can you imagine a mystery novel where the writer states that "the butler did it" in the very first sentence? The controlling statement in a mystery novel, which is so conventional that it is often implied rather than actually stated, is "who did it?" The controlling sentence also provides the framework and main organizing principle for the entire book.

It's OK in your introduction to keep the reader in a bit of suspense. You need to tell him or her what your essay is all about, but you don't need to spill all the beans at once. Say, for example, that your essay is on the impact of the aging population on the design of cars. In the introduction, you probably don't want to state what the impact will be; instead raise this issue as a potentially interesting one. Try to hook the reader. Once hooked, the reader will want to continue reading in order to learn what will be the impact of the aging population on auto design, as argued by you and supported by evidence you have unearthed.

A common mistake of novice students is to brainstorm a thesis statement before they've even done any research, and then to try to make all the evidence they find support that thesis sentence. The Greeks had a god called Procrustes who did the same thing. He got a bed and, when it turned out to be too short, he cut off his legs to fit into it. Don't make yourself a Procrustean bed!

Your essay's body

You can literally count the number of paragraphs that you need in your essay by adding up three things: 1) your major arguments, 2) your main ideas, and 3) the concepts that you need to develop. The rule of thumb is that you usually need at least a paragraph for each concept you need to develop. We'll have a lot more to say about concepts in the next chapter. In the meantime, we'll confine ourselves to their organization.

If you've done that research well, you should have all of these concepts already organized in a mind map or on index cards. It's not a bad idea to put the concepts on sticky notes so that you can move them around as you begin to write. No matter how thoroughly you've organized your research, the process of writing will result in a further reorganization of your thoughts. Sticky notes allow you to play with concepts without being stuck (if you'll pardon the pun) in one permanent location.

The structure and size of each paragraph depends on what you need to write to develop each concept. Don't worry about having short and long paragraphs, just as long as you feel that you are covering the territory adequately. At the same time, it typically happens that you find yourself a little thinner on some concepts than others. This experience may mean that you need to go back to your sources and flesh out the concept a bit more.

Concepts are linked together to form ideas and arguments. Your primary guide in deciding whether or not your information and ideas are developed enough is the logical sequence of your argument. As you compose the body of your essay, you should be constantly reading and re-reading paragraphs to make sure that they flow logically from and to one another.

You can determine whether or not your essay flows by asking the following questions:

· Can I move backwards and forwards logically from any point of view?

· Can I diagram my essay quickly on a blackboard or a piece of paper?

· Can I add greater subtlety or complexity without detracting from the logical flow?

It's equally important not to confuse clarity with mediocrity. We expect university writing and a university audience to be more sophisticated than the reader of pulp fiction. In the film *The Big Chill*, one of the characters is a tabloid writer who never makes his article any longer to digest than "an average bowel movement." You can legitimately expect a higher degree of concentrated attention from your university instructors and your professional colleagues.

Your essay's conclusion

One of the genuine tragedies in otherwise intelligent and well-composed essays is a poor conclusion. Many students sabotage their essay by doing one of the following:

> · stopping without concluding ("thank God it's over!");
>
> · introducing some new idea that hasn't been developed in the main body of the essay ("Oh, by the way...");
>
> · being ambivalent or wishy-washy ("I'm confused.").

The first of these offences is perhaps understandable. By the time you have developed all your points, you feel like your mental work is complete. Wrong! You need to tell the reader succinctly what you think you have proven, or at least underline its significance. There's nothing more irritating for the reader than an essay that builds towards, but does not achieve, a climax. This is the academic equivalent of people who don't finish their sentences but assume that you know what they were going to say.

The introduction of a new idea is inexcusable. You may have other issues that you would like to talk about, but your essay is not the time or place. The only undeveloped issue that you are permitted to mention in the conclusion is the direction that future research on your topic should take.

Mentioning something new in your conclusion takes your readers' minds totally off what you've tried to prove. This is the academic equivalent of the *Friends* episode where Ross says "I accept thee Rachel in sickness and in health, in good times and in bad, till death do us part." The problem was that he was marrying someone named Julia.

Usually students (and writers in general) decide to add new information and ideas at the end because they've discovered something new and perhaps important while finishing up their essay. The secret, or not so secret, means to avoid this situation is to not write the essay at the last minute. That way, if new ideas do occur to you, or you find interesting new information that you are convinced is valuable, you still have time to integrate them within the essay itself. But the best strategy is to learn to feel free not to use them altogether.

If you don't learn how to let go as a student, you will surely learn it when you enter the world of work. Employers simply have little patience for anything that is irrelevant or underdeveloped. They will tell you that, if it is important, you should be showing them how or why, rather than wasting their time making them guess.

Another way to avoid adding new information in the conclusion, is to have a tightly focussed or narrow topic, question, problem or dilemma that your essay deals with. A general, vague and broad controlling statement will, quite naturally, give rise to too much information than can easily be included in your essay.

Why do some students get ambivalent at the end of their essay? Maybe it's because they want to play it safe because they might be wrong. Maybe it's because they really don't believe what they've argued. In either case, an ambivalent ending is a let down for the reader who has followed your argument from the beginning to the end.

You will know that you have concluded effectively if you are able to achieve a sense of closure when you read over your conclusion. The feeling for yourself and your reader should be one of *been there, done that*. Avoid leaving any loose ends!

Let us tell you that there is zero tolerance for ambivalence in the business world. If you compose a case study for your boss, you dare not sit on the fence. People in business have to make hard decisions within strict timelines; they don't have the luxury of fence sitting. So it's a good idea to start getting your ass off that fence now!

Professional documents

Most professional documents are read differently from academic essays in that sometimes only their introduction and conclusions will be read carefully. The meat of the report is usually skimmed or browsed by busy senior executives. That's why it's good practice to be clear, concise and precise in your introductions and conclusions.

Although your TAs and professors will read your entire paper, it is still required that the conclusion of your essay follows logically and clearly from your introduction. You can be certain that both your introduction and conclusion are strong and complete, when you can read them both (without reading the body of your essay) and comprehend the essence of the essay. Moreover, if some points are obscure or confusing in the body of your essay, a strong introduction and conclusion will help to carry your reader through your argument.

Professional documents usually have an executive summary. You can practice writing these by writing and submitting abstracts for your essays, even if abstracts are not required. Not only will this give you practice in the important skill of summarizing a long document into a few hundred words, but you will also impress your professor or TA and, perhaps, earn higher grades.

ESSAY WRITING AS A PROCESS

Essay and report writing is a process, not a mysterious conception that happens the night before a deadline. That process is illustrated as follows:

The first draft

The first draft of your essay or report is the place where most of the hard work is done. It's the place where you integrate thinking, research and writing to craft an argument that:

· establishes a clear thesis, or problem or dilemma;

· addresses and solves a legitimate problem;

· demonstrates that you know how to use evidence effectively;

· reflects your own point of view;

· establishes one or more memorable points (for yourself and your reader).

It's not easy to accomplish all of these goals. At certain points in the draft stage, you will probably run into some mental roadblocks. When this happens, you can help yourself out by:

1. jumping to a different part of the essay where you think the writing might flow more easily;

2. taking a break, relaxing, and allowing ideas to come without forcing them;

3. completing mechanical things like your title and reference page;

4. writing down what you know for now; not worrying about what you don't know;

5. talking to a teacher or colleague about the section you're wrestling with;

6. going back and doing some more research.

The most important thing you can do is to learn to relax without putting your essay completely out of your mind. As long as even a small part of your mind remains connected to your essay, your subconscious mind will be working on the problem and you'll often find that the solution will just come to you. If you try too hard, you don't give your subconscious mind a chance to solve the problem for you. If you let go of the problem altogether, it may be even bigger when you come back to it.

It's a very good idea to get into the habit of carrying around a notebook where you can jot down insights as they come to you. Experienced professional writers do this as a matter of course. Many even have a pad and pencil on the nightstand next to their bed for any revelations that come in the middle of the night. Nothing is more annoying than going back to sleep and finding that your idea has evaporated completely by the next morning!

The second draft

A great writer was once asked the secret to her success. Her answer was immediate, simple and pure. Rewriting. If you were to apply a cost-benefit analysis to essay writing, spending a day rewriting your essay has the biggest payoff. Here are some tips to guide rewriting:

- always leave a couple of days before you compose the second draft of your essay; while it's too fresh in your mind, you won't be able to spot any problems objectively;

- examine what you've written as though it were a classmate's essay rather than your own work;

- now is the time to pay particular attention to the transitions between paragraphs; are these transitions smooth and helpful to the reader?;

- read your essay out loud to see if it makes sense and flows when spoken.

Reading your essay aloud is an extremely effective communications strategy. Here are a few of the things you can discover about your paper simply by reading your essay aloud:

- its overall effect, tone and flow;

- whether it's focused or unfocused;

· where the gaps are;

· the ideas that work and don't work;

· how often you repeat yourself.

This strategy can be even more effective if you use a tape recorder to tape the reading and then listen to the playback. Modern micro tape recorders are cheap, effective and a good investment.

It is not a good idea to focus on spelling or the rules of grammar during this stage. Once you begin to word by word edit, you completely lose your ability to engage in creative problem solving. You also lose the ability to look at your essay from the point of view of an interested reader rather than a marker with a red pen.

The final draft

The final draft is the right time to do the close editing that every paper needs. This is the time to go over grammar, punctuation, spelling and word choice. Software programs have certainly made the final editing process a lot easier than formerly, but they can miss and mislead. It is up to you to perform that close and careful check that makes the difference between many B+ and A essays.

Students often wonder why they get penalized for mistakes that have nothing to do with thinking. The answers are simple:

· spelling and other mistakes are signs of sloppiness;

· a limited vocabulary prevents you from saying what you really mean;

· poor punctuation detracts from the flow of your essay, forcing the reader to go over sentences more than once;

· weak grammar reduces the force of a sentence and often changes its meaning.

There is little tolerance for grammatical mistakes when you write anything for an organization or company. Your superiors don't get paid for locating and fixing your spelling mistakes. If document goes out from a company or organization, and a client or reader spots a grammatical mistake, it can be very embarrassing.

Editing

It is very difficult, and often impossible, to edit your own essay. It is hard to find the problems, both grammatical and substantive, in your own writing. No author can possibly edit his or her own work expertly.

With editing you need to enlist the help of your colleagues. In a professional environment you would likely be working in a group, and so many editors would be available. For an essay, you should try to have two sets of editors: one set for the second draft to give you advice on problems with logic, structure, arguments and so forth. A second set of editors will be needed for the final draft to look only at writing problems.

A common mistake is to ask family and friends to read over your essay. These people will want to be supportive and are likely to report back "darling, this is the best thing you have ever written." Such comments are not helpful. Find colleagues who are critical, who will question you, who will point out flaws, problems, inconsistencies and so forth. When you find such people, or when you have trained them, treat them very well. Their effort is guaranteed to increase your essay grade considerably.

By the way, the best way to find good editors is to reciprocate. They will give your papers as much attention as you give theirs. If you are not as good a writer or editor, reciprocate in other ways.

Many blue-chip companies have collaborative strategies for editing important letters and documents. All such need to be seen and commented on by several different people at each stage of the writing process. Each person is expected to take their editorial responsibilities extremely seriously, and the group as a whole comes under scrutiny if someone doesn't do their job properly.

Citing sources

A problem that many essay writers have is how to cite material, from books, articles and the web. The general rule is that you must reference both ideas and facts that you acquired from other people, whether you copy these word-for-word or summarize them in your own words. If you are copying material (that is copying and pasting) you must place this material in quotation marks so that it is clear to the reader that these words are not yours.

Unless you are directed to use one particular citation style, either that developed by the American Psychological Association (APA) or the Modern Language Association (MLA), the key is to be consistent. If you start with one style, then use it throughout the entire paper. If unsure, just adopt whatever style is being used by your textbook, or other key books or articles, in the course.

Perhaps the easiest style is to use parentheses in your text. Let's look at an example. You cite another author's idea in three different ways in your text:

> Other authors argue that mandatory retirement is discriminatory as well as ineffective public policy as it will result in labour shortages (Gillin and Klassen, 2000).

> Gillin and Klassen (2000) specifically argue that "forced retirement based on age is discrimination" (p. 42)

> One position is that "forced retirement based on age is discrimination" (Gillin and Klassen, 2000, p. 42)

In your list of references, the following would appear:

> Gillin, C. T. and T. R. Klassen. 2000. "Retire mandatory retirement," Policy Options, vol. 21, no. 6, pages 39-62.

If this article was obtained from the web, then the only change is how it is presented in the list of references:

> Klassen, Thomas R. 2000. "Retire mandatory retirement," Policy Options, vol. 21, no. 6, pages 39-62. Retrieved June 27, 2003, from the World Wide Web: http://www.irpp.org/po/archive/jul00/gillin.pdf

Citing sources completely and accurately is extremely important in government and business, where an infringement on intellectual property rights could result in an expensive lawsuit. At the very least, the failure to cite sources completely will be very embarrassing if brought to the attention of the media.

A case in point. The government of Great Britain recently released a document providing evidence for weapons of mass destruction in Iraq. It turned out that the document was largely plagiarized from an unacknowledged source – a CIA document. Not only was a department in the British government guilty of copying the work of others. But, also it was guilty of presenting, as factual truth, the argument of an organization that was anything but impartial and probably decidedly biased.

You can bet that some of the people responsible for putting out that document lost their jobs. They may have thought that they were supporting their Prime Minister, Tony Blair, but they ended up bringing an entire government into disrepute.

Don't forget the title and...

When you perform your final edit, don't forget the title of your essay. Every essay, regardless of its length or content, should have a meaningful and interesting title. A title should not be a rewording of an assignment question but should give the reader some insight into what you say in your essay. Just as the eyes are the mirror to the soul, so too a good title should mirror your argument.

Along with the title, comes the title page that includes basic information such as the date, course number, your name and student number, the name of the professor or Teaching Assistant. Make the title page interesting (maybe with a diagram or graphic) since it sets the tone for the remainder of the paper. It is always a good idea to ask your teacher if they have any specific preferences, however, since some do not like diagrams, graphics or unusual fonts.

At this stage you may also want to consider - if you have not already - whether an interesting quotation might be suitable on the first page of the essay. Many authors find this a good way to gain the attention and interest of the readers. You may have noticed that we use this approach in our book. All of our quotations were chosen carefully for meaning and relevance. Last, but not least, also make sure that you have numbered the pages in your essay.

COMMON ESSAY WRITING ERRORS

If you think you need extra work in English grammar, you should actively seek help from your university's writing centre or a private tutor. Do not hesitate to do this, as you will quickly improve your writing skills and your grades!

Some common writing mistakes in both university and professional writing include:

Overuse of the passive tense

Sometimes it's difficult to avoid using the passive tense. Overuse of the passive tense, however, significantly reduces the clarity and force of your sentences. Students often use the passive tense to avoid having to identify the subject of a sentence. For example, a student might write, "This was seen to be an important issue." A good marker will ask: "by whom?"

Pronouns and persons

Always check your pronouns to make sure that the antecedent references are correct. Many students have a tendency to mix up persons and to jump between the singular and plural case. Also, be sure to avoid vague pronoun references, such as "it". For instance, "It was good last night" leaves the reader speculating what it was that was good. For an eighteen-year old male, "it" almost always refers to SEX!

Tense confusion

Perhaps the most common, and most distracting, grammatical error is the incorrect use of tenses. This forces the reader to go back over the sentence to make certain that they have read it correctly. If you begin the essay in the past tense, you need to continue in this tense (unless there is a logical reason to change it). In any case, always be aware what tense you are writing in.

Run-on sentences

Almost every undergraduate essay has at least one run-on sentence. A sentence is a complete thought with a subject and predicate. Once a sentence is complete, you need to put in a period and start a new sentence. You can occasionally separate very closely related thoughts with a semi-colon, but it's best to use a period. You can always use *and* to add more phrases, but the longer the sentence, the more you should refrain from the practice.

Convoluted phrasing

There are many causes of convoluted phrases, such as the complexity of the idea or the confusion of the writer about what they want to say. But, a common, and unnecessary, cause of convoluted sentences is the attempt to sound academic. By attempting to sound academic, you usually come off as *pedantic*. A pedant is someone, usually a professor, whose inflated language makes him a pompous pain in the ass. Hopefully, you won't get too many of these professors at York, and certainly not in the Division of Social Science!

This error is often combined with the use of the passive tense, making sentences even more unwieldy. Aim to be as clear as possible, and remember that although something may sound clear to you, it is the reader who counts.

Incorrect choice of words and missing words

This is usually a sign that a student has written their paper in a hurry. It is like telling your teacher (or employer) that you wrote it at the last minute. It usually conveys that old familiar expression – "I don't really give a shit!"

Trust me, you don't want to leave that impression; so it's important to re-read your essays or reports at least one last time before handing them in.

"Sounds fine to me", "I wasn't marked wrong for this in high school", "I think the professor or teaching assistant is being way too picky."

No one likes to be criticized for their writing, especially if they have not received such criticism before. We've got news for you; you're not in high school anymore. University and the workplace can be very critical.

We've had some students look at the red ink on their marked papers and complain that their papers are "bleeding"! You can be certain that your managers, clients and colleagues will be far more harsh and direct in their feedback than will your professors. In most large companies or organizations, no letter or document goes out until it has been edited and re-edited at several levels to avoid anything remotely unprofessional.

Progressive organizations can also be very rewarding to those who possess good writing skills. Really good writers, like really good thinkers, are increasingly rare commodities. Good writing skills can take you far in your chosen profession.

Possessive use

Many students, and others, have difficulty with the possessive form. With a little practice, it will become easy. Remember that a plural is different from a possessive and does not require an apostrophe. The "tails of two cats", therefore, is different from "two cats' tails". Note that the apostrophe usually comes after the *s* in the case of plurals and before the *s* if the possession is singular.

There are always exceptions that complicate any rule, especially in English. Perhaps the biggest confusion is between "its" and "it's".

its = the possessive form.
"The company failed to meet its profit targets. The cat chased its tail."

it's = it is; it has.
"It's a well paying summer job as a work study student at York."

Common spelling errors

Some errors are made more often than others. Remember the following:

compliment = to say something nice
(He paid me a compliment about my report)

complement = to fit together
(Her work complements my work)

principle (noun) = a rule
(A principle of the legal system is that ...)

principal (adj.) = most important
(The principal character in the play is the mother)

principal (noun) = a person in a position of leadership
(A principal heads the school)

affect is usually a verb meaning *to influence*
(My gender affected my chances)

effect is usually a noun meaning *result* or *consequence*
(The effect of the treatment was...)

effect is sometimes a verb meaning *to bring about*
(I will effect a change in my life)

Lab reports and similar assignments

In the above sections, we dealt primarily with writing essays; however many of the same comments apply to other types of writing that you may be asked to do in university, whether it be book reviews, journals, or case studies.

A lab report is something of an exception. These are fairly restrictive and formulaic, so make sure that you have a clear idea of what is required and don't wander out of the accepted parameters.

Case studies are more concise and business-like in style and have an organization all their own. They move rapidly from description and analysis towards an optimal solution. The case study method has serious limitations. However, there is still enough room to explore alternatives and to demonstrate critical and even creative thinking.

The last word

In this chapter we have given you specific tools and suggestions on how to improve your performance on different types of exams and written assignments. Use these as applicable to improve areas of your school-work that you are dissatisfied with. However, remember that you need over time to develop a style or method that works best for you, and gives you the results you desire. The more your style or method is honed during your days at university, the more you can expect that it will serve you well after graduation.

Disneyland wasn't built overnight. Expect learning to write well to take considerable time. But, also be aware that there are few skills with as big a payoff in the workplace than the ability to express complex thoughts in written documents.

NOTES

[1] T.G. Gebremedhin and L.G.Tweeten. 1994. *Research methods and communication in the social sciences.* Westport, CT: Praeger, pp. 92f.

CHAPTER FOUR

DEVELOPING YOUR CRITICAL SKILLS

By three methods we may learn wisdom: First, by reflection, which is noblest; second, by imitation, which is easiest; and third by experience, which is the bitterest.

Confucius

INTRODUCTION

The workplace of the future will continue to be characterized by change. Modern organizations, no matter how small, need employees who do more than carry out duties competently. They need team players who can share, filter and process information effectively. The kind of skills that you should be acquiring at university and that are the keys to long-term success in the workplace are known as critical skills. Any progressive employer will want critical, as well as professional skills.

The primary vehicles for organizing knowledge critically are *concepts* and *theories*. Concepts are the building blocks of theories, and theories are abstract analytical frameworks for understanding data. Together, concepts and theories provide powerful tools for discovering meaning. Classical economics, for example, is an abstract and ideal theory of markets. The key conceptual building blocks of this theory include self-interest, competition, private property, profits and *laissez-faire*.

Concepts and theories come in many shapes and sizes, and like the world we live in, they change all the time. Being able to adopt and adapt concepts and theories well is what makes the difference between a merely average and a really good student or professional. So it is well worth the time and effort mastering them.

But we are getting a bit ahead of ourselves here. Before delving more deeply into concepts and theories, we need to get a better handle on this notion of critical skills that your professors and future employers seem to take so seriously.

WHAT EXACTLY ARE CRITICAL SKILLS?

Don't be misled by terminology. Some students seem to think that having critical skills means always criticizing things. Nothing could be further from the truth. In fact, you could just as validly call critical skills *constructive* skills, providing that you realize that constructing new solutions always presumes the ability to take outmoded structures apart or *deconstruct* them.

One sure sign of intellectual immaturity is the tendency to criticize without being willing to reconstruct. Your professors likely will be more tolerant of negativity than your employers because they know how necessary, yet unfamiliar, it is for students to question received knowledge and assumptions. But, ultimately, critical thinking has to be constructive and strategic if it is to be of any professional use. The slogan "if you are not part of the solution, you are part of the problem" applies to critical skills.

Critical skills are the tools and strategies that we use to creatively analyze, compare, synthesize, and communicate information in order to resolve confusions and solve problems. These skills are prized in every society, but they are essential in modern life where we privilege intelligent and imaginative thinking as the keys to progress. The primary purpose, indeed the rationale, of university education is to cultivate these skills in future leaders and professionals.

Your university studies are designed to build disciplinary and professional, as well as critical skills. Of the three, however, critical skills are the most important for lifelong learning because they transfer to the widest range of activities. Scholarly disciplines and professional requirements change all the time. Concepts and theories are also subject to change. But the critical skills required to organize concepts in relation to theories remain constant over time and do their work in all cultures. Professional and disciplinary competencies may provide you with an entry-level job, but your success in that job will depend on critical skills.

Critical skills are essential to human and organizational flourishing. Without critical skills, human societies would have no control over the changes that affect them. They allow us to:

- identify problems and make intelligent decisions;

- make connections and formulate hypotheses to resolve confusions;

- compare and contrast the implications of particular strategies;

- evaluate and communicate a preferred outcome;

- act confidently and decisively.

THE CONNECTION BETWEEN COMMUNICATIVE AND CRITICAL SKILLS

Problem solving is the heart of critical thinking, but communication is its soul. So important is communication that we are going to delay talking about problem solving until the next chapter in order to explore the connection between communicative and critical skills more thoroughly.

If you can't communicate clearly, you can't think critically. Sounds a bit harsh, doesn't' it? Students occasionally complain to us, especially when they get an undesirable mark on an essay or presentation, that they are being treated unfairly because we marked their writing rather than their understanding. But when we go over their assignment critically and constructively, it usually turns out that they didn't really understand the issues very well at all.

Good communication skills make for good critical thinking because they provide students and employees with the symbolic and structural tools to define and solve problems with clarity. Communication, especially in the form of dialogue or debate with others, has been regarded as a primary catalyst for thinking at least since the ancient Greeks. With the invention of paper, writing became the primary medium for developing and conveying critical skills. This is why essay writing remains such a fundamental part of a university education.

One of the reasons why we hold critical and communication skills in such high esteem is because they are not easy to cultivate. In terms of biology and cranial capacity, we are an intelligent species, but we can also be mentally lazy, suggestible, emotional, habitual and prejudiced creatures. Not only do we need to work hard to cultivate our critical skills, but also we need to work even harder to apply them consistently and continually. The phrase "use it or lose it" applies to critical skills.

Do you know why people with advanced university degrees don't get Alzheimer's as often or as early as the general population? It's certainly not because they are genetically superior. It's because they typically work in professions or for organizations where they are required to practice communicative and critical skills.

Students often assume that communication just means talking to others and, hopefully, interesting, entertaining or convincing them. Inexperienced students often fall into the error of trying to communicate information in ways that they hope their professor will approve. What they fail to understand is that communication does not only take place with respect to others. Learning to think critically involves *communicating with ourselves.*

We communicate with ourselves all the time, but our self-communication typically has a lot of *static* and is full of misleading or contradictory meanings. When we talk to ourselves, usually our habits or our feelings get in the way of real understanding. Critical thinking is the method for eliminating static and communicating more meaningfully with ourselves. The most successful people in any profession, and in life generally, are those who have learned these skills.

There are three fundamental ways that communication relates to critical thinking:

1. Communication skills allow you to *clearly* identify problems and issues; if you are able to symbolize a problem, you are already well on the way to solving it.

2. Words are symbols. The symbolic dexterity that comes with good communication skills allows you to probe an issue more deeply.

3. Communication skills are needed to connect symbols or *concepts* to theories. Concepts are the building blocks of theories and theories are the most sophisticated ways of organizing knowledge.

Most people have a superficial understanding of problems and issues; they tend to believe whatever they are told or whatever is easiest to understand. Most people jump too quickly to simplistic solutions that are a *dime a dozen* because they lack the capacity to symbolize effectively. Their loss is your gain. You have an opportunity to set yourself apart, and to provide value-added information and analysis to your chosen profession or organization, by developing your critical skills.

DEVELOPING YOUR CRITICAL SKILLS

Nobody ever said it was easy to develop your critical skills. If it were commonplace, there wouldn't be such a demand for people with those abilities. But many writers on critical skills make it a lot more difficult than it has to be by throwing tons of abstract *stuff* at you and hoping that some of it will stick. A better approach is to begin by recognizing that you've always had the capacity for critical thinking; you just didn't have the knowledge to focus those skills effectively until now. The trick is to practice more rigorously and systematically the kind of thought processes that you've performed intuitively in the past.

Our goal in this chapter is to make some of the *invisible* rules behind critical skills more visible for you, so that you can try them out for yourself.

Before beginning your journey, here is a tried and tested piece of advice about critical skills. Almost no one learns critical skills effectively by trying to *memorize* all the rules. As Michael Gilbert suggests:

> Like trying to remember someone's name, the harder you try, the more difficult it becomes; but, as soon as you give up, relax, and stop trying, the name comes to mind...The information is there, you have been accumulating it; by *relaxing and listening*, you allow the mind to react freely to what is heard. A similar situation exists in sports. You can learn all there is to know about the correct tennis or golf swing, but *thinking* about your right arm while on the court or links is the worst thing you can do. Instead, a coach will recommend you relax completely and clear your mind.[1]

Learning critical skills is like learning a professional sport; it is difficult but that doesn't mean that it has to be unpleasant. There are few things in life that give as much satisfaction as successfully solving a mental problem. Really nailing the argument in an essay or composing an effective report is a lot like making a great golf shot. Making sense of a complex issue that you might have once considered beyond your skill is like reaching the green from the rough.

The most important of all critical skills is the ability to *identify key concepts and ideas*. Far too many students and employees are passive. They approach learning situations like open vessels expecting to be filled. Because of this, they have trouble sorting out the key ideas from the other facts that they are taking in. When thinking critically, you have to separate out the important concepts from the examples or the evidence used to support them.

You use concepts all the time, probably without realizing it. Concepts are symbolic inventions designed to aid understanding. Concepts don't come out of the air. They are cultural inventions. The concept of adolescence, for example, was an invention of the nineteenth century; before that time teenagers simply didn't exist. The concept of the *peer group* to which you belong, was invented in the twentieth-century by social scientists.

Peer group is a concept or symbol that has a *definition* that it might be useful to know more about. Dictionary and encyclopedia definitions are useful but usually limited. There is a complex body of scholarly and professional information on peer groups that make the concept more analytically useable. You probably have an intuitive understanding of your peer group, but do you know all of its characteristics? Demographers, marketers, teachers, actuaries, criminologists and many other professions have *unpacked* the concept of peer group in fascinating ways. For example, advertisers try to manipulate your insecurities and your need to simultaneously belong to, but stand out from, the crowd.

Concepts rarely get used in isolation. In order to make them more useable, we tend to organize them in clusters and to distinguish between those that are more fundamental (sometimes called independent variables) and those that are more secondary (sometimes called dependent variables). What is fundamental and secondary usually changes depending on the particular issue we are looking at or the problem that we are trying to solve. Thus, we may be trying to understand peer group pressure as a dependent variable of adolescence or we may be researching adolescence as only one example of peer group pressure. Other forms of peer group pressure might occur in crowds, religious cults, suburban environments (keeping up with the Joneses), etc.

Concept clusters can range from the relatively simple to the much more complex. Concepts in the academic disciplines, for example, tend to be organized within sophisticated classificatory systems. You might think that you know what is meant by a concept like *democracy*. But I guarantee that you will have a much more sophisticated understanding of that concept cluster if you take a course in political science. The social scientist Lawrence Neuman, suggests that democracy is a concept cluster with at least 3 quite separate dimensions:

1. free elections with everyone having a vote,

2. freedom of expression and association,

3. a government controlled by an elected legislature.[2]

Within and between these three dimensions, there are many different variations that political scientists study.

You might notice that the definition of democracy provided by Neuman doesn't say anything about free enterprise or capitalism, something that people often associate with democracy. Concept clusters invariably make *assumptions* and often exhibit distinctive *biases*. But some assumptions and biases may be necessary to make the concepts work while others could be entirely *unwarranted*. A genuinely democratic society, for example, need not be capitalistic; it could just as easily be a socialist state.

THE LIMITATIONS OF NARRATIVE

Human communities have always organized and passed on important information in the form of *narratives*, plots or stories. There is nothing intrinsically wrong with this; narratives are valuable ways of knowing as well as important sources of information. They are essential to personal and cultural identity. But there are serious limitations to constructing knowledge along story and plot lines.

We've noticed a tendency among younger students to try to make information meaningful by organizing it within a narrative. When asked to do research, they can be very good at providing you with the basic plot and think they have provided added value if they give you lots of details. But relatively few beginners are good at dissecting and illuminating the fundamental *meaning* or *significance* of the story.

Most of our students like movies, so when we teach critical skills we often use films as examples. You can watch a movie superficially, in terms of its narrative plot, or you can watch it critically. A good movie should communicate meanings. At least some of those meanings will be invisible to those who only want passive entertainment or an entertaining plot. A truly great and lasting movie will challenge your assumptions by providing subtle and complex meanings. If you are accustomed to thinking critically, a movie that relies solely on a romantic or ingenious story line may seem like an insult to your intelligence.

The movie *Pretty Woman* starring Julia Roberts and Richard Gere, admittedly well acted and moderately entertaining, is relatively *meaningless* because it doesn't have very deep or interesting messages. It trots out some rather trite beliefs like: 1) romance conquers all obstacles; 2) there's a Mr. Right somewhere for every woman; 3) everybody has an equal opportunity for happiness. This combination only becomes remotely plausible if you look like Julia Roberts and have the good fortune to have a benefactor who is also a millionaire. Moreover, most millionaires tend to look more like Bill Gates or Donald Trump than Richard Gere.

When we say things like this, our students sometimes complain that we are being too cynical. They legitimately argue that most movies are pleasant stories in which we suspend our disbelief. That's fine as far as it goes, and at least shows some degree of critical separation. But many people live their entire lives within these fantasies and make very poor marital and career choices as a result. Some people even feel like failures when their lives don't work out like the movies. They often lack the critical skills to cope effectively with what life offers them.

To put it bluntly, lots of our students lack the ability to detect the crap that Hollywood throws at them. The plot of *Pretty Woman* is loosely based on a play by George Bernard Shaw called *Pygmalion*. Shaw's play offers readers or spectators much more sophisticated and ambiguous meanings. One of Shaw's messages is that romantic illusions are not necessarily fulfilled and may even be *ideological* to the extent that they mask or excuse some fundamental social problems. Furthermore, he argues that economic and educational inequalities need to be seriously addressed if the phrase *equality of opportunity* is going to mean anything. You don't necessarily have to agree with Shaw to recognize that he provides some worthwhile food for thought.

You would be amazed at how many people lose a good movie's meaning by focusing solely on its plot. The trouble with working at a deeper level is that meaning may not be obvious and can often be multiple. What is most *critical* to critical thinking is locating the *key concepts* and *assumptions*, and recognizing in advance that they may be both complex and multiple. This means that you have to be prepared to work at and dig deeply into the material to find the nuggets that may not be apparent. Not all materials contain nuggets. *Pretty Woman* doesn't have much to offer other than passive entertainment. But you can bet that your university level readings and assignments will.

Being critical means recognizing and assessing levels of meaning. A *bone fide* critical thinker is someone who can tell you what the best movies are and give you good reasons why. Almost all film (if its good it's often referred to as a film rather than a movie) critics, for example, think that *Citizen Kane* is one of the great American movies. Why? It's because it is a film that delivers many levels of meaning. It's a narrative based on the history of a rich American newspaper baron. It's also a moral drama that shows us how power and wealth can corrupt. It's an allegory on the rise of the American nation from innocence to complicity. It's a study in ambiguity that illuminates the complexities of a human being rather than a black and white *stereotypical* image. Finally, it's an artistic masterpiece that uses metaphors in a very sophisticated way to deliver complex meanings.

The more closely you concentrate on *Citizen Kane*, the more you get out of it. In fact, most people miss at least some of the movie's levels of meanings the first time around. While you may get more entertainment value out of *Terminator 2* or *Sleepless in Seattle* than you do out of *Citizen Kane*, there is no comparison in terms of depth, technique and significance.

CONTEXTUALIZING INFORMATION

Being able to identify key concepts and ideas is important, but you also need to be able to compare and contextualize them. In the original play

Peter Pan by J. M. Barrie and in several various movie adaptations, we are presented with a combination of key ideas:

1. The importance of the creative imagination.

2. The inherent goodness of people, i.e. the innocence and creative potential of childhood.

3. The need to retain the child in the adult.

4. The need for children to grow up and take responsibility for their actions.

In the play *Peter Pan*, the key idea or primary message was probably number four. In the movie, *Hook*, the key idea was probably number three. In the most recent movie, *Finding Neverland*, the key meaning was probably number two. This shift in focus makes for a very different *emphasis and meaning* even though the basic plot may be similar.

The difference between *Peter Pan* the book and *Hook* the movie leads us into a very important component of critical skills — the *context* of the information. Key ideas and concepts are *foreground* information; but in order to determine them, we often need to take into account the *background*.

The background can take different forms. In the case of *Peter Pan*, we might want to take into account the author's intention. The author was a Scotsman living during a time when the British Empire was at its height and the ideal values of society were patriarchal, military and masculine. While he might have regarded childhood as a wonderful and formative period (the place where moral ideas are constructed), the author likely believed that adults (particularly males) needed to take responsibility for their actions and play an active part in governing an extensive empire. There was a time to be a child and a time to grow up.

Steven Spielberg's movie *Hook* was produced at a very different historical period. For many Americans in the 1990s, their lives seemed to be becoming more bureaucratic, materialistic and disenchanted. Many yearned for a return to the more childlike and innocent values of rural America (as interpreted by Walt Disney). Thus, we see Peter Pan (aka Robin Williams) not needing to learn to grow up, but to regain his childlike innocence and imagination. The plot and characters are essentially the same, but the primary *message or meaning* could not be more different.

Context includes a lot of things that can provide us with clues as to meaning. It can include the time something was written (*history*), what we know about the author (*biography*), and the type of writing or material we are looking at (*literary genre or scientific paradigm*), or the socio-political position of the author (*ideology*).

Context is only one way of determining meaning and can sometimes be misleading. Besides, it often limits our understanding of and appreciation for a given issue or work. One of the most important *clues* to meaning is the use of concepts that function more as *symbols* than definitions within a classificatory system. A fascinating distinction between works of literature and social scientific writings resides in the former's more imaginative use of symbols to convey complex, subtle or ambiguous meanings. While metaphorical symbols certainly are not lacking in the social sciences, the requirements of systematic analysis tend to limit their use. In works relying more on *imagination,* symbols are used much more commonly and creatively as *metaphors.*

In the novel *To the Lighthouse,* for example, the author Virginia Woolf continually refers to waves, different kinds of waves, on the ocean. Sometimes the waves are mere ripples and all seems secure and serene. Sometimes the waves are choppy and distinct from each other. At one point in the novel, the waves are beating viciously against the shoreline. It helps a lot if you use your critical skills to recognize that the descriptions of waves have little to do with any plot or story, but a lot to do with the author's meaning. Waves symbolize human relationships. Human beings are connected with one another in the social ocean. But waves also connote individualistic separation. Consequently, human beings are sometimes connected with one another and sometimes apart. Occasionally, they come into fundamental conflict (World War I in the novel) and the human community is transformed into a stormy and threatening ocean.

Thus, in Virginia Woolf, the symbol of the waves is a *key to meanings in the book*. If you were paying attention to all the varying descriptions of the waves, you would have a much better understanding of what this great work of literature is all about. Good luck looking for a plot or a story. There simply isn't one. In great works that rely partly on a more traditional narrative approach, you can still find an attention to symbols. In *Citizen Kane*, for example, the protagonist's (main character) dying word is "rosebud". Rosebud, if you watch the movie very, very closely, is the name painted on his child's sleigh, when Kane was so full of promise.

To discover the meaning of any book, article, essay or work of art, it is important to look at the *title*. Literary authors often use key symbols of meaning in their titles. One of Virginia Woolf's other novels was simply called *The Waves*. The title of Sylvia Plath's novel *The Glass Bell Jar* tells you a lot about the message that she wanted to convey. The work is about a highly intelligent woman in a society where women are not allowed to develop their own identities and often end up in suffocating relationships with males. A *glass bell jar* is an inverted glass dome that scientists use to measure how long it will take mice or insects to use up the limited oxygen in a confined space. What does that tell you about Plath's message? Why do you think Plath is such an inspiration to feminist writers?

Important symbols can be found even in the most seemingly scientific works. Copernicus referred to the Greek image of a lantern in the center of the sky to help readers re-imagine a world where the planets revolved around the sun. In order to assist his readers in visualizing the workings of the free market (where supply and demand are in equilibrium), Adam Smith used the image or metaphor of an *invisible or hidden hand*. This symbolized the fact that the market would make everything right if only it was left alone.

Smith needed the support of this symbol because almost no one in 1776, when he wrote *The Wealth of Nations*, had ever dreamed of a free market and had a difficult time visualizing one. Once a symbol is used, it becomes available for adaptation or even inversion by others. Many economists view the *hidden hand* as Adam Smith's primary meaning for their discipline, whereas Smith might have been using it merely to support his preference for less regulated markets.

In order to understand what Adam Smith was saying, therefore, you might need to take both *symbols* and *context* into account. You might also want to recognize that other writers appropriate or invert symbols for their own reasons. The modern economic historian, Alfred Chandler, played upon Smith's symbol in the title of his book *The Visible Hand*. What do you think it was about? How does the modern economy work? Who has the power to direct or manipulate the market? Chandler's message is that we no longer operate in a free marketplace; increasingly global corporations control our lives as well as the risks of the modern market.

THE SIGNIFICANCE OF THEORIES

Chandler has a *point of view*. He thinks that corporations are too big and powerful in modern society. Adam Smith had a point of view. He believed that progress was only possible if capitalists were forced to compete in the marketplace without too much government interference. Virginia Woolf wanted to advise her readers to appreciate the moment and the little pleasures in life, because these were the most human and tangible things we could experience in a confusing and occasionally chaotic world. Sylvia Plath also had a *perspective* or point of view. She was a feminist writer in some important respects, even if she would probably have rejected the label *feminist*. She believed that intelligent women were stifled by, and suffocated in, a male dominated society.

A point of view or a perspective is a *theory*. There's nothing intrinsically mysterious about theories. They are just useful abstractions that combine, order and differentiate related concepts for explanatory purposes. In fact, you use theories all the time. If you think that Bill Gates must be smart because he's so rich, you are invoking a theory (however dubious) that economic success correlates absolutely with intelligence. Same thing when you say "if you're so smart, how come you're not rich." There may not be much data to support your theory, and interpreting the data could be problematic, however.

An academic theory is very careful about the way it uses data and formulates claims about that data (the so-called *facts*). Scholars are expected to be scrupulous in processing information, to limit their claims to what the data supports, and to continually test their abstractions against the available evidence. Scholars usually only apply the term *theory* to highly integrated, tightly argued, and logically warranted explanations.

There are some theoretical distinctions between the sciences and the liberal arts (i.e. social sciences and humanities). In science, many, but not all or even the most important theories are expressly *predictive*, while in the social sciences and humanities theories tend to be more *explanatory*. But the differences between various kinds of theories and points of view are less important than what they have in common. In essence, they all involve primary or sufficient causes for certain events or outcomes. They are all ways of making sense of a bunch of data that would otherwise be much less comprehensible or useful.

Acquiring critical skills means not only thinking more deeply but also more expertly. Demonstrating expertise implies having a *bag of tools or techniques* that will help you mine more deeply and probe for diamonds. The tools or techniques that are most valuable for probing data are *theoretical* approaches or *frameworks*. Many of these theoretical approaches are available within academic disciplines or the professions. Let's say, for example, that you wanted to understand how critical skills usually develop among your fellow university students or peers. Then you might want to adopt a theoretical framework developed by a man named Benjamin Bloom. Bloom's developmental analysis goes like this:

1. First year university students tend to see the world in black and white. They want teachers to tell them what's right and wrong. They take in information passively and uncritically.

2. By second year, students begin to realize that the word is *gray* rather than black and white. At this point, they understand that meanings are multiple and that *facts* need to be interpreted. While they understand the significance of *viewpoints*, however, they are not so adept at handling theoretical frameworks.They tend to become relativists and to think that they, and everyone else, is entitled to their opinion.

3. By third year, students begin to deploy theoretical frameworks more adroitly and learn to back up their arguments logically and with evidence. However, the weakness of this stage is that they probably still lack a coherent world of personal meaning with which to process the information that they receive. They have learned to think more critically, but they are still dependent upon their teachers.

4. With a little luck, by fourth year students have well-developed theoretical frameworks of their own which they apply *independently* to material. They recognize diversity, but have the ability to form and integrate materials for themselves. They no longer look to see what the professor thinks, but are able to approach texts and other materials independently.

Bloom's psychological taxonomy is not a dogmatic account but a theoretical framework for understanding mental, personal and ethical growth.

A *theory* is a systematic way of interpreting or making sense of reality. While they have explanatory or predictive power, rarely do theories claim the status of absolute truths, even in fields such as physics and chemistry. Rather, they are useful ways of organizing a more complex reality. Not every first year student will think as stereotypically as Bloom suggests. Not every fourth year student will be as mature and independent as Bloom hopes.

Just because theories are *critical tools* doesn't mean that they are therefore inoculated (immune) from critical analysis. Feminist scholars, for example, have criticized Bloom's taxonomy, for its gendered one-sidedness. Feminists suggest that Bloom's taxonomy is a fairly accurate vehicle for measuring male development. However, it is not so good at describing female psychological development and maturity. Can you guess how a feminist scholar might criticize Bloom's model? Can you think of a different model, or even variations to the model? If so, you are already demonstrating a capacity for critical thinking.

THEORETICAL LEVELS AND FORMS

Theoretical frameworks take a variety of forms and operate on a number of levels. To put it as simply as possible, there are: 1) big, overarching theories that explain huge chunks of reality (Meta or macro theories); 2) theories that explain small, local phenomena (Micro theories); and 3) in-between or intermediate theories that link big and small theories (Meso level theories). Most of the time, people operate either in terms of big or small theories. But, a Meso level theory is sometimes invoked to explain an anomaly or a problem in a macro level theory.

Are you getting lost? Here's an example. The Marxist theory of economic development is a Meta theory that predicts a revolutionary conflict between the working class (proletariat) and the owners of the means of production and wealth (bourgeoisie or capitalist class). If you want to retain the theory but explain why a revolution has not occurred in the twentieth century, you might want to use a Meso theory that describes ways that employers and governments have used combinations of rewards (higher pay, and programs such as Employment Insurance) and controls (surveillance, threats of outsourcing) to prevent workers from organizing more effectively and bringing about the revolution that Marxist theory predicts.

Bloom's taxonomy is a fairly low level (Micro) theory that is an adaptation of a larger theory (Meta) of cognitive development by the psychologist Jean Piaget. Large overarching, or Meta, theories have been extremely important and fundamental ways of organizing knowledge and under-standing data in the liberal arts and social sciences. Such Meta theories include: Marxism, Freudianism, Feminism, Existentialism, Pragmatism, Deconstruction and Postmodernism. These *really big* theories often incorporate many aspects of human existence including psychology, spirituality, economics, philosophy, sociology and ethics. Sometimes Meta theories are compatible with one another; more often they are mutually exclusive.

Meta theories and their master theorists have fallen on hard times recently. We *postmoderns* are more adept at deconstructing and fragmenting than unifying our reality. In music, we used to have three categories: classical, jazz and popular. Now we have hip-hop, rap, classic rock, alternative, adult alternative, world, electronic, industrial, and that execrable stuff that they play on elevators.

But Meta theories and theorists will always have a certain popularity or *cool* factor for three reasons: 1) because they provide considerable explanatory power, 2) because they can completely transform the way you look at data or reality (i.e. they are often counter intuitive), and 3) because it takes a hell of a lot of critical skill to learn them well. Let's face it, if it takes that many years to learn something, you are not going to be easily convinced that it's useless. Scholars have spent their entire lives exploring Freud's theory of the Id, Ego and Superego. There is a large group of Marxist academics that continue to refine and update his theory of dialectical materialism. There's an entire school of Derrida scholars in Departments of Literature who will try to convince you that there is no such thing as an author only abandoned texts that leave differential traces of meaning.

You are not expected to become experts in these theories during your undergraduate years. But learning to think critically will involve learning some concepts and approaches from these theories because they are such useful tools. For example, Karl Marx suggested that human history should be understood as the *conflict* between groups or social classes. If you use this theoretical approach, you should be prepared to examine historical materials for evidence of such struggles, such as revolutions, strikes, etc. Sigmund Freud illuminated the power of the subconscious mind. You will find lots of evidence of his influence in modern novels and movies like *Momento* that explore the mind using such techniques as *stream of consciousness* and *mental flashbacks*. You don't have to completely understand existentialism or Jean-Paul Sartre's complex discussion of consciousness to appreciate some of his insights into our modern crises of meaning. Everyone who has had to make difficult ethical choices, who has observed the many hypocritical ways that we tend to rationalize our selfish behaviors, or who has ever felt that "hell is other people" can take something from the existentialist canon (body of theories).

Some major theories in Sociology

Every field or discipline will have its own particular favorite theories. In Sociology, four of the major ones are very briefly reviewed below, with the key concepts in italics.

Structural functionalism — a Meta theory that proposes society is a complex *system*, composed of many *structures*, such as the family, school, government, employers, each with a specific *function* that achieves *consensual equilibrium*

Translation: modern society is both fair and efficient

Conflict theory — a Meta theory that views society as a fundamentally *unjust* and *unequal* combination of *classes* with *opposing interests*, and where the dominant or *hegemonic* class *exploits* the *labor* of others

Translation: modern society is unfair for most and ultimately dysfunctional

Exchange theory — a Micro theory that suggests all human interactions have an *economic character* in that people operate on *self-interest* to obtain *rewards*, including *approval* or affection from others

Translation: everyone is out for himself or herself and life's a negotiation

Symbolic interactionism — a Micro theory that people construct their *self* and create *meanings* from interacting with others, including role-playing and using symbols (primarily but not exclusively language)

Translation: you are a symbolic variation of what you see

At this point, you might be thinking: this is all very well and good but what does any of this have to do with life after university? If so, you really haven't fully grasped the enormous power of theoretical thinking.

At the minimum, simply by being able to work confidently with theories implies that you will be able to detach yourself from the increasing and overwhelming flow of information and to form useful abstractions. A theoretical facility will make you a much more effective sifter and processor of information in an age when these skills are becoming the most essential. Even if you don't buy the whole theoretical package, you will find some of the concepts generated by these theories indispensable.

Big theories will seem irrelevant if you don't know how, when and where to apply some of their tools. For instance, Sartre can tell our corporate executives a lot about why they should accept responsibility for their decisions. He can also show corporate critics how some executives practice habitual *bad faith* with shareholders and stakeholders. Max Weber's theories about large organizations and Freud's analysis of civilization can help someone in a Human Resources department understand why employees become unhappy in unnecessarily bureaucratic and rule bound situations, and why workplaces might need to pay more attention to the mental health of their employees. Marx is indispensable to anyone with a serious interest in the causes of worker alienation and distrust of employers. Even someone as esoteric as Derrida, taught properly and with a minimum of jargon, can assist those working in global and multicultural environments to reach beyond their eurocentric perspective and learn to respect and embrace cultural differences.

The significant differences and incompatibility between some of these major theoretical perspectives often frustrate novices in theory who want to know "which one is right". These differences, however, turn out to be real advantages for anyone interested in their more practical application. Applying different theoretical perspectives to the same problem is an extremely effective way of discovering interesting angles, strategic possibilities and novel solutions. You don't have to buy into a total theoretical package in order to use it to clarify issues and solve problems.

Just remind yourself that no single theoretical perspective will ever be able to completely capture the complexities of human life and relationships. The world and any given individual are too multifaceted and complex to be explainable by any one theory. Indeed, this complexity suggests that multiple perspectives are necessary to understand our environment and ourselves. Those who expect any one theoretical perspective to cover all eventualities may be really *deep*, but they are often inflexible and one-dimensional. You just want to get the fruit that sophisticated theoretical approaches have to offer.

Even if you don't have many opportunities to formally use Meta theories after you complete your undergraduate career, the interpretive facility and depth of thinking that you have learned will be portable to any profession. The stronger your critical (i.e. theoretical) skills, the more employable and successful you will be. There is less question, however, that you will need to demonstrate mastery, and keep abreast of any Meso or Micro theories that are relevant to your profession. Over the past forty years, for example, managers of organizations have had to learn several new theories of the firm, including 1) human relations, 2) quality circles, 3) total quality management, and 4) flexible networking. It is difficult to think of any really challenging future occupation in which you will not need to continually update your knowledge to be successful. Lifelong learning will involve keeping abreast of the latest theoretical approaches in your profession or occupation.

That's why it is important to begin blending theory and practice now. Look for opportunities to relate the latest theories that you are learning to practical problems in the real world. Students in the authors' courses have opportunities to apply the most up-to-date theories in conflict resolution, business ethics, and regional development to real world issues like the Canadian-American trade disputes, the recent breakdowns in the Anglo-American corporate governance, and the future direction of the World Trade Organization. Graduates who take their theoretical know-how to the workplace, and keep it fresh with advances in the field, will be real assets to their employers.

Your university professors don't really expect to turn you into abstract theoreticians (although it may occasionally seem that way). We'll let you in on a little secret; even professors sometimes have a hard time keeping up with new theories. But we'll also guarantee that, with practice, you'll become increasingly adept at deploying them in combination or tailoring them to specific situations and problems.

SOME PRACTICAL TIPS TO HELP YOU ON YOUR WAY

Possessing critical skills is what being smart really means. Some people naively believe that intelligence is something either you have or you don't. Way too much is made of IQ or MENSA scores. We've got good news for anyone who has ever felt stupid. Critical skills can be learned! If you read this chapter carefully, you are already well on the way to developing your critical skills.

Here's a little test. Can you tell me why *Blade Runner, 2001 A Space Odyssey* or even *The Matrix* (the original not the sequels) are better movies than *Star Wars*? Can you tell me why the Beatles' album *Sgt. Pepper* or Radiohead's O.K. *Computer* are more meaningful than anything by the Backstreet Boys, Destiny's Child or Britney Spears? To understand and be able to articulate the difference is critical thinking. It doesn't mean that you have to *like* the Beatles better than Madonna. All that is expected is that, as you develop your critical taste, you will learn to distinguish and appreciate more sophisticated and more deeply layered material.

You don't change from being uncritical to being critical overnight. It is a gradual learning process. That's why a university undergraduate program takes at least four years; it's designed to develop your critical skills. Too many university teachers, however, seem to believe that you can develop your students' critical skills simply by exposure and osmosis. If you hang around long enough, you'll begin to *cotton on*. But you can be much more proactive and systematic about developing your critical skills.

The first step is to begin to *make linkages between what you know and the materials you are exploring*. Everybody has to start from somewhere, and your experience is the best starting point for you. When exploring new material, one of the best things you can do is to *engage* it. What does it mean to you? Do you agree with it? If yes, why? If not, why? You will understand and appreciate more sophisticated materials better if you can relate to them in some way.

But that's just a starting point. Too many students find sophisticated material difficult, different, and challenging. The natural tendency is to over simplify it to make yourself comfortable or reject it because it is different from anything that you are used to. At this point, therefore, it is absolutely crucial to *suspend judgment* and *explore the material as fully as possible*. One of the jobs of university professors is to give you material to study and explore that is rich in symbols and meanings. You will impose unnecessary barriers to learning if you reject this material in an offhand fashion because it is unfamiliar or uncomfortable. In order to develop your critical skills, you need to be prepared to do a lot of work up front. You are like a miner. If you just extract information, it is like mining for coal – useful but not very profitable. If you hunt for concepts and deeper meanings in the coal, your chances of finding a diamond (crystallized coal) are considerable.

Working with theories can seem difficult, but theories are the best mining tools designed by some of the world's smartest intellectual engineers. Don't expect theoretical arguments to read like magazine articles; their purpose is not to entertain but to analyze and instruct. Don't be put off by the technical jargon either.

A note on jargon

Don't fear jargon. It's only words. You already use tons of jargon all the time with your friends. The function of disciplinary (scholarly) jargon is that it allows scholars to condense and compress a lot of ideas or complex concepts into a single word or a combination of concept clusters. Terms like sexism, bureaucracy, hegemony, social class, ideology, cognitive dissonance, hegemony, Protestant ethic, peer pressure and even something as ubiquitous as *culture* were invented by social scientists or liberal arts scholars to communicate ideas more effectively. And let's be honest, using jargon correctly makes you a member of a special club.

Over time, as your critical skills develop, none of this will seem so difficult, and your enjoyment in creating meaningful knowledge will make your work a lot more pleasurable. The thinking process that appears so hard now will become second nature. You will find yourself *discovering* all sorts of things that a critical intelligence has the ability to reveal. The indispensable first step is to suspend judgment and engage in exploration. The results will be worth it.

Developing critical skills is more like running a marathon than a hundred yard dash. Persistence and practice really do pay off. Unlike most physical skills, however, critical skills can be practiced all your life and will enrich it immeasurably.

NOTES

[1] Michael Gilbert, *How to Win an Argument*, (New York: John Wiley, 1966), p. 52.

[2] Lawrence Neuman, *Social Research Methods: Qualitative and Quantitative Approaches*, (Needham Heights, MA: Allyn & Bacon, 1994), p.38.

CHAPTER FIVE

PRACTICAL PROBLEM SOLVING FOR SCHOOL, WORK AND LIFE

Look and you will find it – what is unsought will go undetected
Sophocles

INTRODUCTION

The critical skills you learn at university will make you a more intelligent and valuable employee. In a perfect world, critical and applied skills would be synonymous. Unfortunately, there often occurs a gap between theoretical learning and practical application that gets in the way of effective problem solving on the job. Many employers complain that new hires have state-of-the-art knowledge, but an inability to apply it to real world situations.

By interest and occupation, many of your professors have a preference for abstract and theoretical knowledge. That does not mean that their research or teaching lacks real world significance. What it does mean, however, is that it is not your professors' responsibility to show you how to get, keep and succeed in the job market. You need to take the initiative for yourself.

In this chapter, we have shifted the focus to the applied skills that will allow you to succeed in a much more competitive marketplace than your parents faced. The skills described will prove useful to anyone, including your professors! They will be all the more effective when combined with the analytical and critical skills described in the previous chapter.

WHY APPLIED PROBLEM SOLVING IS SO IMPORTANT

Your employers will be looking for evidence of real world problem solving skills. While the capacity to solve problems may be an innate human trait, the ability to solve complex problems is what separates an *extraordinary person* from an *ordinary person*. People with the ability to solve problems stand out from their peers, are admired by others, and sought out by employers. There is sometimes a tendency to view this ability as mysterious and the mark of a superior intellect or *genius*.

There is a proverb that holds true when it comes to problem solving: *genius is 10% inspiration and 90% perspiration*. The ability to solve complex problems is hard work. You have to take the time to define the problem, identify the root causes, mentally explore possible solutions, and choose the best solution. Even then, your work is not done, because you need to implement the solution and evaluate whether or not it works.

You would be amazed at how many people in positions of authority or importance try to take short-cuts or rely on gut hunches when it comes to problem solving, with often predictable results. To be sure, occasionally your intuition will get you through, and you should never ignore it. But the percentages are against you if you rely on intuition, guesswork or – the worst enemy of all – false assumptions.

What happens when you don't problem-solve properly? First, you waste valuable time and resources doing things in a less efficient way. Second, you usually *band-aid* problems, rather than fix them. Third, many of your efforts will become habitual responses and self-reinforcing assumptions, taking you further and further away from the optimal solution.

In today's highly competitive business and organizational world, there is less and less room for such a waste of energy. Those who try to solve problems based on false assumptions, habit or precedent will be surpassed by those who know how to identify and fix the problems that occur. That is why many modern corporations now identify problem solving as one of the key characteristics that they are looking for in new employees. But you don't need to limit problem solving to business.

Problem solving is a life-skill. We all face problems in our lives. If we fail to identify and act on the root of our problems, we are doomed to failure in terms of self-discovery, healthy relationships, and reaching our goals.

By learning to problem solve intelligently, you can improve your chances of success in your profession and in your life. Applied problem solving is not only one of the best investments that you can make but also, in comparison with other investments, it's relatively simple and straight-forward. It takes years to acquire a university education or professional accreditation, but you can begin implementing your improved problem solving skills as soon as you finish reading this chapter.

PROBLEM SOLVING AS A PROCESS

The single biggest obstacle to successful problem solving is the tendency to rush to a solution. There is something about problems that makes people very uncomfortable and the best way to restore their comfort zone is to come up with a solution almost immediately. Thereafter, individuals have a tendency to cling to their solution and even to defend it aggressively against better solutions.

Consider, for example, the nature of most high school debates. The teacher poses a problem (questions or issues are really problems in disguise). Students identify positions. Quickly the positions become rigid and the debaters become dogmatic. Those who appear to *win* the debate are usually those with the most forceful personalities or the best command of the language. Only rarely, and only in the hands of good teachers, do these debates cause individuals to seriously reconsider their initial assumptions. Moreover, classroom debates, however pleasurable they may seem to the participants, rarely provide new or deeper insights into the problem.

Problem solving at higher levels may feel unnatural at first. It means going slow and being careful. It requires *suspending the rush to judgment* that might obscure the real complexities of the problem and prevent possible solutions. It means being at least as concerned about the route as the destination. It means mapping out that route with care. And it provides results!

Consider the commonplace criticism of male vacation driving habits by women. Many women think that their boyfriends or husbands like to drive by intuition rather than to consult a map or to ask for directions. What often happens on such occasions is that people get lost, waste a great deal of time, and become unnecessarily agitated. Eventually, someone has to ask for directions or retrace the route in order to get to where they are going. This holiday scenario is a fairly simple example of the lack of effective problem solving skills. The consequences are not very serious. Eventually, the partners will retrace their steps and get to their destination. Hopefully, their relationship will not suffer too much.

In life and work, the lack of effective problem solving skills can be much more serious. If a husband and wife have problems communicating, for example, they may assume things about one another that will eventually destroy the relationship. If a manager assumes that the reason his employees are unproductive is because they are lazy, when the problem is really one of inadequate tools or motivation, he can bring down morale and even ruin the company. If a financial company decides to invest the majority of its clients' funds in real estate, simply because there is a temporary boom in house or office sales, it could destroy the retirement plans of hundreds of families. These or similar scenarios happen every day.

The potential seriousness of the consequences of inadequate problem solving are a good reason to opt for a *model* of problem solving that avoids the typical pitfalls of most decision making. Within this model, the *primary process* that we advocate is one that involves *expanding* and only later *contracting* the problem.

If we were to begin by trying to limit or quickly solve the problem, we would be doing ourselves a disservice. In the first place, we would be artificially narrowing the scope of investigation, obscuring the possible causes of the problem, and limiting our ability to gain insights into the issue. Only once we have explored the problem in some detail, and deferred judgment on the solution, should we begin to focus in more tightly on the root causes.

In the initial stages, the most important thing is to identify the problem and possible causes from as many angles as you can. One of the most efficient things that you can do at this stage is take some time out to do a little research. If others have already studied this problem, why not get the benefit of their wisdom? It is well worth exploring the theoretical literature. As we pointed out in the last chapter, the most sophisticated problem solving tools are concepts and theories. Are there any concepts or theories that apply directly to this problem? Are there any theoretical frameworks that could be adapted to explore this problem more deeply?

One of the most effective ways of researching or brainstorming a problem is as a member of a group or as part of a team. That's the best way to get as many opinions on the table as possible. The most effective problem solvers are not people who work on problems in isolation, they are those that look for as much input as possible. Ideally, the team members will have different academic or life backgrounds and will bring different theoretical perspectives and personal orientations to bear on the problem. If you need to address a problem in relative isolation, then the best strategy is to try to be as open to the problem and its potential causes as possible and to explore as many alternate viewpoints as you can.

One of the main pitfalls to effective problem solving, and decision-making in general, is the failure to involve those who could provide the most valuable input into the problem. This mistake has been made all too often by corporate executives who fail to consult with those who have more detailed knowledge related to the problems, such as area managers and functional specialists. Sometimes, those with the most valuable input can even be employees with the least amount of power, such as those who deal with customer complaints on a daily basis. No one is suggesting that a modern corporation is a democracy, but a CEO who fails to solicit input from all relevant employees is probably not a very good problem solver.

In the early stages of problem solving, function is much more important than form. You don't want too many rules; you want to encourage brainstorming and alternative positions. While you can use diagramming – like the fishbone diagram outlined below – these are simply tools to help visualize the problem rather than rules. Once you have sufficient data, however, it becomes much more important to process the information in a rigorous way. Now you will want to be more strategic in the ways that you move towards a solution to your problem. You will be *contracting* the information in ways that are increasingly precise.

Too many people think that the problem is solved once they come up with a solution. But the process of problem solving doesn't end with a solution. Now you need to decide how the solution is going to be implemented and identify who is going to be responsible for its implementation. And you're not finished yet. Problem solving is a continual and open-ended activity for three reasons. First, you can't be sure whether or not you've really solved the problem until you have some hard evidence of your success. Second, real life is messy. While you may have solved your initial problem, new problems can arise as a direct result of your solution. Success in one area can lead to problems in another area. So you need to determine what the *negative as well as positive outcomes* are. Third, the world is continually changing, and this is especially true in our modern global and information society. So you need to continually assess both the problem and the solution to see if they are still relevant.

STEP ONE: Defining the problem

Defining a problem should be a fairly simple exercise, right? Wrong! You would be surprised how many different interpretations of a problem there can be unless the *problem is defined clearly and agreed upon by those primarily concerned with its solution.* There are three characteristics that are essential to defining a problem well:

1. Make the problem as objective and factual as possible.

2. Avoid any ambiguity in the statement of the problem that can be open to misinterpretation.

3. Define the problem in such a way that it is solvable.

Consider the following problem statement:

High school students are unprepared for university because they haven't been taught to read or write well.

The above is a problem statement often made by your university instructors. It is a bad problem statement because it contains implicit assumptions that could get in the way of finding a solution. These assumptions are:

1. The real problem is in the high schools. *This assumption already implies a cause, thereby precluding other possible causes.*

2. Students need to be taught better in the high schools. *This assumption implies a solution, i.e. that high school education needs to change.*

What if the high schools are not the main cause of the problem? Can you think of other possible causes? Doesn't this statement of the problem seem to absolve your university professors of responsibility for helping you to develop the skills you need to succeed at university?

The offending, but commonplace, problem statement is also problematic because it does not encourage those who have identified the problem to fix it. In order for a problem statement to be useful, it needs to be solvable. Nothing in the problem statement as it stands offers university professors any guidance on helping their students to read and write better.

Another unproductive problem statement, this time from the world of business, might be:

> The North American electronics industry is suffering because some Asian countries are allowing companies to dump subsidized products on our domestic market.

Notice that this problem statement assumes that the cause of industrial decline is 'dumping', thereby eliminating other possible causes such as higher quality, advanced features and better marketing. Also, notice that this problem statement assumes an implied solution, i.e. getting governments either to subsidize domestic manufacturers or retaliate by establishing tariffs against imports from countries like Japan. Finally, notice that, like the statements of some university professors, this problem statement makes the problem unsolvable at least at the level of North American electronics manufacturers.

How could we reword the problem statements above to make them more effective? Well, we could make them more objective and factual, eliminating implied causes and solutions. If possible, we could *beef up* their factual nature by making them measurable. Finally, we might frame them in such a way as to encourage people to want to solve them. This is not as easy as it sounds, especially if you want to make the problem statement as clear and concise as possible. That's why it's a good idea to have as many people involved in the creation of a problem statement as possible.

Without the benefit of your input, here's how we might have reframed the problem statements listed beforehand:

40% of first year university students either fail or drop out of at least one university course.

The market share of North American electronics manufactures fell by 15% between 1990 and 2000 while that of Japan and Taiwan increased by 35% and 20% respectively.

Hopefully, the preceding problem statements are:

· clear and concise

· contain no obvious assumptions as to causes or solutions

· can be easily agreed upon

· identify a real problem that can get *buy in* from everyone

· provide some rationale for solving the problem

Clearly, if 40% of first year university students fail or drop out, and everyone agrees that this is too high a number, those in positions of responsibility will be encouraged to develop strategies to decrease that amount, perhaps by offering more student support, mechanisms for the early identification and support for students in trouble, and more critical skills components in courses. Similarly, if a decline of 15% in the market share of North American electronics manufacturers is considered too high, strategies could be devised for increasing that share. The inclusion of the figures on Japan and Taiwan encourages domestic manufacturers to examine *all* the causes for the success of the Japanese and Taiwanese, not merely assuming that dumping is the reason.

You could also *beef up* the problem statement by *including a goal*. The best thing about including a goal is that this focuses the attention of all concerned on outcomes. The dangers of including an explicit goal within the problem statement, however, are that 1) the goal could be unrealistic or unachievable, or 2) the goal could be unnecessarily restrictive or obscure other possible options.

Here's how you might rewrite the problem statements to include desirable goals:

> 40% of first year university students either fail or drop out of at least one university course. Within a 24-month period, we seek to reduce that number by 25%.

> The market share of North American electronics manufactures fell by 15% between 1990 and 2000 while that of Japan and Taiwan increased by 35% and 20% respectively. By 2007, we intend to reclaim 5% of our lost market share.

Notice that we've attached a specific date to achieve our goals. Again, this focuses everyone's mind on the seriousness of the problem and encourages him or her to help solve the problem within a realistic timeframe. Not all problems admit of a rigid timetable, of course, so it might be best to differentiate between long-term goals that could be more fluid, and more specific short-term and measurable steps towards those goals.

STEP TWO: Discovering causes

We use the term *discovering* deliberately here. Finding the causes to a problem resembles an exploration more than an exercise in logic. Initially, logic is not the best tool because you want to keep your options open. Logic wants you to tighten and restrict your causes, whereas your goal is to be as *inclusive as possible*.

First, you want to list as many causes as you can of the problem, not eliminating anything, no matter how silly it might sound. A good way of diagramming this *brainstorming exercise* is a *mind map*. Simply, write down as many ideas as you can. Then go through and see which ideas are connected and draw connecting lines between them.

Next, begin to organize those ideas a bit more systematically. Here, you could use a *fishbone diagram* to help you organize *major and minor causes*. A fishbone diagram resembles the skeleton of a fish. Along the spine, you can have as many bones as you want, and radiating out from those bones can be lesser bones. It is a good idea to divide the main bones into categories in order to make them easier to organize.

For example, in the case of the electronics industry, we might have a fishbone model that emphasizes:

· Financing

· Manufacturing processes

· Logistics and distribution

· Design features

· Marketing

· Customer Relations

· Joint government-industry strategies

In the case of first year university students, we might discuss:

· The lack of critical skills development

· The different learning styles of modern students, i.e. more visual

· Time management and other organizational problems

· Students working full-time jobs while doing university courses

· The lack of effective university-high school liaison

Your work is not yet finished! While still in this step, you need to move towards identifying the *primary causes*. This step involves *judgment*. Whereas we advised you against rushing to judgment prematurely, presumably now you have sufficient information to *weigh the alternatives*.

Notice that how you weigh the importance of these causes has enormous consequences. If you decide, for example, that the main problem facing first year university students is their need to work part or full-time to finance their university education, you will move in a very different direction than if you believe the key problem resides in the need to accommodate the different learning styles of today's students. Here, applying a Marxist theoretical framework might be enlightening. Marx suggested that unequal access to economic resources is the major problem or source of conflict in capitalist society. Unless the fundamental economic problem is dealt with, most solutions will take the form of temporary or band-aid solutions.

Some primary causes can be related to other subordinate causes. For example, if hours working are interfering with students' ability to cope with university studies, better time management skills could be beneficial to them. But that's a very different *kettle of fishbones* (if you will pardon the pun) than saying that the primary cause of student failure is their lack of time-management skills. If many of today's students work full-time while going to university, they presumably have better time management skills than we ever did as students. Adopting a Marxist theoretical perspective might allow you to recognize the inherent *bias* in approaches that blame the victims for their own victimization.

How do you identify primary and subordinate causes? One rather simplistic way is to construct something called a Pareto Chart, which is really just a fancy-pants name for a graph that diagrams the percentages (out of a 100) that you would attach to any particular cause. But that doesn't really address the heart of the causal issue.

In order to find the primary or *root* causes, you have to subject each of your causes to a *battery of why questions*. In other words, you have to repeatedly ask *WHY* until you get as close to the bottom of the matter as possible. Let's try this with the problem of systemic failure among first year university students.

Why do so many first year students fail or drop out? Answer, because they lack the critical skills required to succeed at university. Why do they lack these skills? They lack these skills for two reasons: because these skills are not provided clearly or systematically in first year courses and because students fail to take the time to develop them on their own.

Why don't students take the time to develop these writing and reading skills if they are so necessary to success? They fail to manage their time effectively either to make use of the resources available to them or to develop them on their own. Why can't they find the time to develop these skills? There could be more than one cause for this. One cause is because many of our students spend too many hours working, which doesn't leave time for their studies let alone the development of their critical skills.

Why do they spend so much time working? Many York University students, more proportionally than from other Ontario universities, come from lower income families and therefore need to contribute more financially to their own education. Are there any other factors that contribute to their dilemma? Perhaps. York is a commuter campus. Getting to York by public transit can be a problem. Students may also be caught in a double bind. They need to work to pay for a car that will get them to and from York and their jobs more efficiently. The irony is that they may then need to work longer hours to finance a car, even more time taken away from study and academic development. Until the issue of student employment is dealt with, any other solutions to the problem will be partial at best.

Of course, you do not need to agree with the assessment above. You might think that York students work long hours to have cars, clothes, cell phones and iPods. Our only purpose is to show you how to ask *why questions* in order to discover the *root problem*. In this case, we identified the root problem as the need for York University students to work long hours to finance both their education and their commute to and from work. This would leave students with less time to devote to their academic development. Even if resources were made available to them in the form of writing workshops, critical skills seminars and personal counseling, they might not have the time or energy to avail themselves of such resources.

Now notice how enlightening such a causal analysis can be. It shows us that York University students face quite particular obstacles that do not exist to the same extent for students at other universities (at least not in the aggregate). Throwing money at student support mechanisms, which York University sometimes does, may not address these particular problems. In York's climate, issues like bursaries, on-line instruction, improved transportation and the like may be more important to student success than well-intentioned efforts that do not go to the *root of the problem.*

The relation between theories and applied problem solving

Theories are systematic vehicles for asking *why* questions and getting to the *root* of the problem. Not only will using theories help you avoid analytical dead ends, but also it will encourage you to clarify any assumptive principles that you might be making.

Problem solving in a theoretical vacuum is a lot like trying to reinvent the wheel. It is a trial and error process that achieves mixed results. That is why it is so important to try to keep abreast of the theoretical literature in your chosen field or profession.

Always remember that theories are the most sophisticated and best-tested problem solving tools and you will save yourself a lot of unnecessary work.

STEP THREE: Establishing solutions

You can clearly identify the problem and its primary causes, but if you don't have an appropriate solution, you will have wasted your time. Ideal solutions are problematic beings because they don't usually have a life of their own. They are governed by all sorts of things like habit, custom, procedure, organizational rules, not to mention such obvious constraints as time and money.

When you were defining the problem and looking for causes, you had relatively few constraints apart from common sense. Once you start identifying solutions in any organization or relationship, you'll find yourself beset by naysayers. That's precisely why it's important to go back to the process that you encountered when you began looking for causes. When looking for solutions, as when looking for causes, you want to be sure to *expand your horizons* before *compressing or contracting them.* Sometimes what seems impossible at first is entirely possible, but only if you are willing to seriously explore it as a possibility. Just because something is initially foreign or unusual does not mean that it might not be a viable solution.

So begin by generating a *longer* rather than a shorter list of options. Use the brainstorming technique to generate the list and include *everything* for the first go around. Here are some tips for brainstorming solutions:

1. Don't judge anything. Most scientists thought that Einstein's Theory of Relativity was nonsense at first.

2. Encourage *thinking outside the box.*

3. Be prepared to go beyond your personal opinions, habits and experience.

4. Explore each solution fully even if you think it's silly at first.

Eventually, you will need to shorten your list of solutions. But before doing this, be careful to document those solutions that work well together.

Sometimes a solution might not seem the best possible one when looked at in isolation but, when paired with another solution, it could provide a powerful tandem.

STEP FOUR: Making a choice

Choosing the best solution means narrowing down the possibilities. You do this, not by looking at each solution and giving it a percentage (as is the case with the Pareto Chart). You need to be much more rigorous than that, given the practical realities that you or your organization faces. The best way to make a choice is to *establish the criteria for choosing*, weigh the criteria and establish something like a point system to measure the various solutions.

Something very much like this is done all the time in large organizations. Unfortunately, it is not usually done at the very highest levels of decision-making but primarily during the hiring process. Human resources departments in large public and private sector organizations generate a list of criteria for interviewing candidates for employment. In that way, they counter the natural human impulse to overlook the real strengths of the candidate based on his or her personality and performance in the interview. By asking each candidate questions based specifically on the hiring criteria, a great deal of bias and personal favoritism is eliminated.

Similarly, if you list five or more criteria for evaluating the solutions, you stand a much better chance of choosing the one that is best for your organization. Such criteria can be fairly straightforward:

1. Cost

2. Ease of implementation

3. Chances of success

4. Extent to which the problem is eliminated

5. Potential buy-in of members of the organization

Each of these criteria needs to be weighed. Chances are you might want to weigh #4 fairly heavily, but maybe not. For example, if by solving the problem, you might alienate many members of the organization, you might want to be careful about the way you weight your options. If *buy-in* is not crucial to your organization's overall strategy or success, you can weigh #5 less than you otherwise might.

Here is a set of criteria that York University might apply to its attempts to address the problem of failures and drop outs among first year students. Notice how different this is from a non-academic corporation.

1. Cost = 25%

2. Ease of Implementation = 5%

3. Chances of Success = 15%

4. Elimination of Problem = 30%

5. Buy-in of Community = 25%

For most market driven businesses, the chances of success and the elimination of the problem would take up a higher percentage. In a public institution like York University, however, other factors could easily be more important. Below is a possible rationale for the percentages outlined above. However, note that it is an administrative rationale, and not one that would find endorsement from students or faculty.

Cost: Cost is a significant issue. University funding from government has decreased in real terms over the last decade, arguably resulting in increased fees for students. While universities should invest more in students, they will need to keep costs under control.

Ease of implementation: This is not such a problem at the University because employees do not have to generate revenue and much of the involvement could be voluntary (students and professors working on committees).

Chances of success: Many university initiatives are long shots and we have become accustomed to failed attempts. As social pioneers, universities can and should take risks. In any case, the institution will not be destroyed if we are unsuccessful.

Elimination of problem: It is more important for York University's administration to be perceived as dealing with problems than solving them. Many of our competitors deal with the same problems with only limited success. We simply have to be, or be seen to be, as good as them. (I realize this may sound a bit cynical! But that's often the way that administrators approach student related problems).

Buy-in of community: This is a much bigger problem at a university than in the business world. Businesses are responsible primarily to shareholders. The university is an intellectual community, to a degree cocooned from the external community. The internal academic community can cause difficulties if it feels that the administration is doing something counter to its interests. That doesn't mean that University administrations lack real power, only that they have to be careful not to polarize opposition on important issues.

We are not suggesting that this is an ideal rationale. It is just an example. The crucial thing here is you have criteria and that these criteria are weighed. Without the weighting, the solution adopted might be different from the one that works best for the organization. By assigning percentages, you are able to marry your organization with the best solution for you. Although it might seem terribly unromantic to some, individuals sometimes engage in this kind of ranking when deciding whether or not to marry a particular individual. Dating services do this kind of ranking all the time. Here, for example, are some possible criteria for a life partner:

· Physical beauty = 25%

· Intelligence = 20%

· Sense of humor = 10%

· Appreciation of nature = 15%

· Compatibility = 20%

· Income = 5%

How would you rank your ideal partner? Do you think that you would make a better choice of a partner by establishing these criteria beforehand? Don't you think you would avoid some problems of incompatibility later on if you gave this some thought?

STEP FIVE: Implementation

Moving from strategic thinking to purposeful action involves some critical steps that are very often overlooked, even in large corporations where ineffective action could be disastrous. In order to *implement* your strategy, you need to develop an *action plan* or *timetable for implementation.* What this means is:

· Breaking the strategy into specific steps or stages.

· Determining the time when each stage should be completed.

· Determining who will have responsibility for ensuring that each step is completed (i.e. specific rather than overall responsibility).

An action plan is a formal document, but until it is fully implemented, it's still more of a blueprint than anything else. It is not a legal document that absolutely requires conditions or contracts to be met. For this reason, those who develop the action plan might also want to develop a parallel *contingency plan.* A contingency plan anticipates possible problems with implementation and develops strategies for dealing with those problems.

You can develop a contingency plan by identifying the things that could go wrong in each major step of the action plan. While the contingency plan will not be as specific as the action plan, it should be more than an afterthought. Moreover, those responsible for implementing the action plan should be familiar with the contingency plan for the following reasons:

- They will know exactly what to do in the event that the plan is delayed or if new circumstances make changes necessary.

- They will be able to make subtle shifts in the action plan to make a smoother transition to the contingency plan if they know the plan in advance.

- They will be more confident that there are options if things don't go according to plan.

- Overall, participants who are aware of the contingency plan will have greater agency (i.e. will take greater responsibility).

One of the mistakes made by authoritarian or *top down* managers who believe too strongly in their own power and need for control is that they keep any contingency plans away from those responsible for implementation. The implication is that the existence of a contingency plan provides subordinates with an excuse for diverging from the preferred action plan. Most progressive theories of management would frown on such a negative approach, particularly with respect to professionals who have as much a stake in the company's success as their superiors.

STEP SIX: Benchmarking and evaluating

How do you know if your action/contingency plans are on target? At the end of the day, how do you know that you have been successful at eliminating/fixing the problem? Many organizations develop and implement elaborate plans but shy away from evaluating their progress.

A typical managerial *con job* is to emphasize partial successes or positive outcomes that are only tangentially related to the actual problem that you set out to solve. In advance, therefore, you need to:

- Establish *benchmarks* by which you will establish progress towards your desired goal (i.e. solving the problem).

- Collect *data* that will demonstrate relative success or failure.

- Establish the criteria according to which you will evaluate overall success.

Assuming that your action plan has been successful, and that you have achieved your goal and solved your problem, you need to do one last thing:

You need to establish some guidelines to ensure that the problem will not recur.

The problem with problems

Most problems are like bad habits; you can think that you are rid of them, but the minute you relax, they will resurface. Given all the hard work that you've done to solve a problem, it is certainly worth the effort to make sure that steps are in place to keep it from recurring.

Let's assume that you are in a problematic relationship with a member of the opposite sex. You could engage in a lot of hard work to identify root problem(s) and either 1) work on a joint solution or 2) extricate yourself from a toxic situation. If you simply reproduce that bad relationship with someone new, however, have you really addressed and solved the problem?

PROBLEM SOLVING AS A LIFE SKILL

Our focus in this chapter has been on applied problem solving for organizations. But problem solving isn't something only done by professional employees. It is something you should be practicing throughout your life. It is an essential skill for deciding and reaching your life goals. It is of crucial importance to building good relationships and dissolving potential or real conflicts with others. Getting to the root of personal conflicts is the first step towards developing a mutually agreeable solution. The popular T.V. psychologist, Dr. Phil, is effective largely because he shows couples and families how to practice problem-solving skills.

It's a good idea to develop this skill before you graduate, if only because prospective employers will be looking for evidence that you possess it. While you might not be able to demonstrate significant organizational problem solving at this stage, you will certainly have some life experiences that indicate your problem solving skills and professional potential. One of the most common job interview questions is "describe a problem that you have had with other people and tell us how you dealt with it." If you can show prospective employers that you have used some of the six steps outlined above in dealing with the complex and delicate situations that occur in most human relationships and job situations, you will be a much more attractive candidate.

Interpersonal problem solving skills are at a premium in the modern workplace, where individuals with different competencies form teams to work on projects. Your demonstrated ability to find common ground with others is an attribute that many of today's employers will value as much as any technical expertise.

CHAPTER SIX

CREATIVE PROBLEM SOLVING FOR LIFE AND WORK

Trust that still, small voice that says, "This might work and I'll try it."
Diane Mariechild

INTRODUCTION

As any self-respecting artist will tell you, creativity is its own very best reward. It enchants our life and makes it worth living. But creative thinking is also a highly prized attribute, especially in our complex modern world. The pace of modern life and its preoccupation with technology reinforces *experiential* and *reactive* modes of reasoning that seduce us "into confusing action for thought and passive entertainment for creative participation."[1] In our over stimulated society, creative thinking is on the decline. Those who demonstrate it are in increasingly short supply.

Some people think that creativity is genetic. Either you're born with it or you don't have it. You often hear individuals say, "I'm not very creative," as if their lack of creativity were cast in stone. The reality is that creativity is something that everyone possesses. Have you ever noticed how creative children are when they play? Imagination makes all things possible for children. They have a remarkable ability to forge magical alliances between themselves and whatever environment they experience. Recapturing that childlike approach to experience can contribute to your happiness and success in life.

Those who suggest that you can't *teach* creativity have a point. Being creative is more about *freeing* something that may have become *blocked* by many years of learning the other valuable kinds of knowledge you needed to make your way in life.[2] It is largely a matter of letting go of overly rigid habits.

What you can *learn*, however, are techniques for letting your creative juices flow. And, ironically, you can learn these creative techniques in a logical and systematic way.

RELATION TO PROBLEM SOLVING

Most problem solving privileges experiential and logical reasoning. It is data driven, deploying conceptual tools to organize and focus the flow of information. Creativity involves developing a different set of skills. It is a fluid and flexible form of *reflective reasoning* characterized by "top down processing". The mind molds reality rather than simply reacting to it. But the mind doesn't exist in isolation and creativity isn't developed in a vacuum. Problem solving is the catalyst. It is the characteristic mental response that changes.

The majority of problems can be solved using the steps outlined in the last chapter. A more creative approach to problem solving is required to deal with complicated problems that don't fit into an established pattern or routine. At these times, it is important to become more spontaneous and uninhibited in your thinking patterns.

What the scientists think

The most recent scientific work on the human brain suggests that *conventional* problem solving occurs primarily in the left side of the brain whereas more *divergent* or creative approaches to reality are products of the right side of the brain. In childhood, we are all "creativity engines" but our talent for divergent thinking is repressed and becomes more difficult over time. The left side of the brain literally takes over.

Conventional intelligence does not equate with creative intelligence. In fact, when the left side of the brain is damaged, as in fronto-temporal dementia, greater creative powers are often unleashed. This happens because logic and memory lose control over some of the brain's functions. This ability to "let go" is a creative characteristic.

Thinking that is over specialized can get in the way of creativity. When *experts* adhere to disciplinary models too rigidly, they tend to lose their capacity for conceptual flexibility. When an accepted methodology doesn't work, these specialists usually find themselves at a "mental dead end". That is why multi and interdisciplinary approaches to knowledge are inherently more creative than disciplinary ones.

Ideally, however, creativity involves a *marriage* of the left and right sides of the brain. The most useful ideas are ones that combine imaginative thinking with theoretical and disciplinary knowledge. For example, Einstein's breakthrough with the theory of relativity was based upon an expert understanding of conventional physics and mathematics.

Source: "Unleashing Creativity," *Scientific American*, Volume 16, Number 1, (April, 2005), pp. 16-23.

Creative thinking is fun. It is inherently playful. That's why children usually have a much greater capacity for creativity than adults. They take the time for mental play and they are highly motivated to be creative. We adults ignore this childlike capacity for mental play at our own risk. The most difficult and important problems that we face in life and work are not always ones that lend themselves to straightforward or logical answers. By taking an overly rationalistic approach, we restrict our ability to find solutions.

Experiential and rational problem solving is a skill that most of us have learned to some degree and one that is very useful in dealing with many of the problems that we face. Many university graduates, but certainly not all, possess this skill. What differentiates creative problem solvers from *normal* problem solvers is their ability to tackle and solve the problems that stymie most people.

Here is an example of a problem that requires a creative solution. Change the following Roman numeral to 6 by adding only a single line:

IX

What stops most people from finding a solution to the problem is that they narrow down the problem artificially. Despite the fact that the number 6 is in the question, they believe that they are confined to the numerical system composed of roman numerals. They forget that there is a completely different system that they can refer to in order to solve the problem. Consider the Arabic number 6. Then think of how you would spell it. Have you got the answer yet?

SIX

Another example requiring creative problem solving is the false equation:

VII = 1

Can you make this a true equation by moving only an I? The answer requires considerable creativity. Why? Because you have to explore – or *play* with – a lot of unusual combinations in order to come up with a solution. Here's a hint: the solution includes the symbol for a square root.

Here's a problem for the numerically challenged. Drop a dime in an empty wine bottle. Then put a cork in the top of the wine bottle. Your task is to get the dime out without: 1) removing the cork, or 2) breaking the bottle. The solution involves thinking outside of your regular mental box. Did you consider pushing the cork down into the bottle? Good for you!

If you didn't get any of these puzzles, there is no reason to feel bad. Most people don't get them, at least not right away. The goal of introducing these puzzles to you is to show you how rigidly you structure your mind and to get you more accustomed to thinking *outside of the box.*

THE RIGID STRUCTURES OF THE MIND

There are several major obstacles that you need to know how to obliterate if you hope to become a creative thinker. Unless you eliminate these barriers, more creative thinking techniques won't have a chance to take hold. You can discover some of these barriers for yourself by thinking of the differences between children and adults that allow the former to be more creative.

Complacency

Complacency means that you are lazy about thinking. You don't want to be bothered. You assume that thinking is too much hard work. This attitude prevents you from exploring your curiosity. Just consider how many WHY questions young children have and how intensely curious they are. You need to recapture some of that curiosity. In order to do that, you have to be prepared to think.

Allow yourself to be curious. Spare some time for thinking. Think about all kinds of different things that seem to have nothing to do with your job, school assignment or your immediate experience. Let your mind wander and explore again.

Fear

Fear is the creative mind killer. Fear means that you are scared of making a mistake or looking foolish. Small children have no such fear and go boldly where adults fear to tread. One of the most creative people we ever knew attributed all of her creativity to the fact that she was not afraid to look stupid.

In order to be a creative thinker you need to be willing to take risks. You need to be courageous. Creative people need to be able to explore lots of options, most of which will be unsatisfactory. The fact that they are willing to look at problems in unique ways means that many of their analyses and proposed solutions will seem strange to others. But they will also be able to provide original, unique and successful solutions to problems that no one else could.

Consistency/Constancy

Oscar Wilde once remarked, "Consistency is the hobgoblin of little minds." What he meant was that people who think in overly linear or rigid terms are not capable of creativity. To be a creative problem solver you need to be able to apply different kinds of thinking to problems. You need to be able to think laterally – looking for associations, similarities, linkages – as well as vertically or logically. You need to be able to picture the problem symbolically and visually and not simply in terms of verbal reasoning.

Notice how limited logic and numerical reasoning were for solving the problems we presented above. To arrive at solutions, you needed to step outside of the box altogether. Getting the right answer isn't the most important thing; stepping outside of the box is.

Stereotyping

Stereotyping isn't always a bad thing. It means grouping things into a category because of perceived similarities. We organize our lives everyday by stereotyping. But stereotyping can be an obstacle to creativity whenever it blurs subtleties or ignores differences. The worst kind of stereotyping is black and white thinking – dividing people and data into highly simplistic and restrictive categories such as right and wrong, good and bad, familiar and unfamiliar.

University education tries to go beyond the stereotyping of everyday life by having you look for subtleties, ambiguities, and differences. Then it gets you to recombine information into completely new, deeper, more complex and meaningful categories.

But a university education can sometimes inculcate limiting stereotypes as well. Overly dogmatic teaching methods, insular scholarly disciplines, and overly rigid theories sometimes prevent new ideas from percolating to the mind's surface.

Compressing/Reducing

We have a natural tendency to reduce any problem that we face into something manageable. In fact, we often do this so quickly that we have no chance to see the problem differently or to explore different options. That's because we are too eager to rid ourselves of the problem.

Being creative involves reversing these habits. You need to expand the problem, look at it in different ways and from different angles. Eventually, of course, you want to try to solve the problem, but you will have many more interesting solutions if you expand it first. You can't be creative if you narrow the problem down too quickly; you can't illuminate the problem unless you look at it from a variety of positions; you can't incubate creative thinking unless you are willing

147

to play with different approaches.

One of the best ways to expand a problem is to examine it through the conceptual lens of a 'theory' (see the last chapter). Many theories are *revolutionary*, not necessarily in terms of advocating radical change, but in *transforming* the way that you look at the world. Being creative involves thinking at the deeper levels that characterizes theoretical understanding. You have to be careful, however, not to lose the 'play' element if you want to apply theories creatively.

A comment on business education

Contemporary business education suffers enormously in our opinion from this tendency to compress and reduce problems. It relies unduly on the *case study* method and *bottom line* thinking. Case studies have a tendency to fossilize information and examples within overly simplistic formulas. The *right* solution is typically imbedded in the problem from the start. Consequently, once business students have a grasp of case study methodology, they usually compose them mechanically and routinely.

The preoccupation with the bottom line (profitability) is extremely short sighted and underscores many of the dilemmas of shareholder capitalism in the Anglo-American business environment. It completely undermines creative possibilities that could contribute to the long-term viability of organizations, not to mention more meaningful working environments.

More conventional problem solving obviously has its proper time and place. But if our business schools really want graduates who are creative problem solvers – as they often say they do – then they need to imbed the possibility for creative thinking more firmly in their curricula. Presently, the business school curricula mimics assembly line instruction in its emphasis on quantity rather than quality. It wastes a lot of predictable energy without providing much illumination.

CREATIVE PROBLEM SOLVING TECHNIQUES

Now that you have a better understanding of what some of the obstacles are, we can begin to discuss techniques for increasing creativity. Remember, *everyone* has the capacity to develop his or her creativity. Originality is much more widely dispersed than most people imagine. The trick is tapping into it. Here's how:

1. The first, and most difficult (but ultimately the most fun) task is to recover our curiosity and wonderment about the world and people. This is difficult to do in our ordinary day-to-day activities where custom and habit have made us rigid. That's why we need to re-engineer the process by reading, thinking and exploring subjects that are less familiar to us. Reading or watching programs on topics that interest us, but are not necessarily *useful*, is one of the best ways to do this.

When we expand our minds on less familiar territory, we give ourselves fresh information to explore in a more playful way. What is surprising, even magical, is the way that this new information invariably informs the other areas of our lives by allowing us to make novel connections and to see new possibilities. Again, don't overlook the theoretical frameworks that you learn at university as potentially fresh ways of seeing and exploring the world.

Sometimes we don't even need external sources of stimulation to revitalize us. If we simply set aside time to think, meditate or just *be*, we can find our minds emptying momentarily, leaving some room for new ideas to come in. If our minds continue to chatter in old accustomed ways, it's hard for anything new and exciting to appear.

It goes without saying that free time is imperative for this process to occur. Having a balanced lifestyle is critical to creativity. The saying "all work and no play makes Jill a dull girl and Jack a dull boy" is entirely appropriate when it comes to freeing your creativity. Incurable workaholics need not apply!

2. Our second suggested technique aims at *shaking up* your customary mental approaches and habits. Because these are so second nature, you really need to practice a mental transformation. You can do this by teaching yourself to *make the familiar strange*. By making the familiar strange, you can see things that you never saw before. Use your imagination to do this, or if you can afford it, travel to a new environment.

An anthropologist once described the ritual behavior of a strange tribe whose male members daily went into a small but brightly lit room. In that locked cubicle, they took a sharp blade and scraped away a layer of skin from their faces. Sometimes during this ritual, the blade was too sharp and their faces bled so much that the blood had to be soaked up with cloths. Despite all the mess and the pain, however, the majority of males in the tribe routinely went through this barbaric procedure every day.

What on earth do you think the anthropologist was describing? Would you believe he was describing the act of shaving in a bathroom? Notice how the act of shaving becomes a strange ritual when made unfamiliar. Now consider the many ways that you can enrich your understanding of everyday experiences by making them less familiar. Most students study and write essays or assignments for at least four years before they are allowed to work at a professional job. How strange is that? When you work, many of you will earn a wage for doing a job between 9 and 5 most days. Many people hate what they do for a living. Isn't that a weird way to live? A medieval peasant or tribal warrior would certainly think so.

And what about shopping for clothes and other consumer durables? That might appear to be very peculiar, obsessive, and psychologically disturbing behavior to our ancestors. In fact, being a *consumer* might not be a very sensible way to live at all! Would someone from the past be able to make any sense out of an expression like "shop till you drop."

A recent film *The Corporation* invites a unique perspective on some large and powerful organizations. Since corporations have many of the same rights as individuals, the film's writers decided to apply psychological theories of personality to these powerful behemoths of modern life. What do you think they discovered? They discovered that some of the world's most powerful corporations have explicitly *psychotic* personality traits. If they were real people, we would likely avoid them and their senior executives like a disease.

3. A third, and very important creative technique, is to defer judgment. We all tend to be too quick to judge what a problem is and to decide what the best solution is. Judging things too quickly is a recipe for uncritical and uncreative behavior. In order to appreciate great art or literature, we have to give it some time, to hold back on judging. We have to explore the problem or subject matter in greater depth. We have to be willing to give the work or the problem a chance to *speak to us.*

Many first year university students have a real problem with this. They either like or dislike things way too quickly. They have a tendency to dismiss difficult literature or creative ideas as boring or unintelligible or both. They need to learn to look upon a new text, a new subject, or a scholarly discipline as a challenge rather than to treat them as consumer choices.

You will never be able to think creatively unless you are able to give problems and issues the benefit of the doubt. You will never be a creative problem solver unless you learn to go beneath the surface in order to explore something in-depth.

It goes without saying, therefore, that creative thinking has a lot in common with critical thinking. Both are the opposite of superficial thinking. Both forms of thinking have the capacity to move deeply as well as laterally. They are rarely passive. Neither accepts information or ideas at their face value, but look for less obvious and even hidden meanings. Critical and creative thinking are both highly *reflective* approaches to learning. The main difference between them is that critical thinking is usually serious and guided by logical rules, whereas creative thinking is playful and willing to dispense with those rules.

4. A related technique involves looking at data or problems from odd or unusual perspectives. That's exactly what Einstein did when he looked at the universe. Before Einstein, most scientists perceived the universe as a big clock where all the parts were connected in a linear fashion by cause and effect relationships. The two unquestioned certainties in this clockwork universe were time and space.

Einstein allowed his mind to make this mechanical universe more fuzzy and problematic. He was able to see space as curved rather than linear. Moreover, he was able to see that time and space might not be constant, but relative to the perception of the viewer. As he put it, a minute can seem like an hour when you are sitting on a hot stove; but an hour can seem like a minute when you are in the arms of a hot date. That's what the theory of relativity is all about.

A more down to earth example involves a collection of community groups who hold an annual parade. Because it was concerned about liability, the city administration passed an ordinance that these groups would have to pay for insurance to cover all future parades. Since these community groups didn't have sufficient funds to pay for insurance, it appeared as though the popular annual parade would have to be terminated.

The ingenious solution that community groups developed was to hold a *stationary parade* in a large communal field. No insurance was necessary as long as the parade was not moving. The spectators did all the moving. The community groups creatively redefined the concept of a parade to make it viable. The annual stationary parade became a social and economic success.

5. Yet another technique that has always been identified with human creativity is the imaginative use of *symbols*. Artists, singers, actors and writers are prized in society – some becoming rich and famous - because they are creativity experts. Instead of trying to present information logically, they use symbols, metaphors, and analogies. Playing with symbols in this way allows artists to visualize the world in deeper, richer and more interesting ways.

A simpler (and admittedly more mundane) example of how to use this symbolic approach is Edward de Bono's *six action shoes*. When faced with a problem, de Bono suggests that we try *putting on* different kinds of shoes to look at the problem differently and symbolically. When we put on our navy shoes, we can think in terms of habit, custom and routine ways of doing things. But when we want to expand a problem and get more information on it, we should try putting on our gray sneakers. Sneakers allow us to be more casual, to take our time, to relax and allow our brains (also gray matter) to work on the problem.

Other shoes include pink slippers that make us feel comfortable, homey and protected. In our pink slippers, we bring our feelings – our hopes, fears, and compassion – to bear on the problem. Brown brogues are the perfect shoes for taking practical action; purple riding boots are ideal for making regal executive decisions; orange gumboots are the attire of choice when entering into dangerous or muddy terrain. The more symbolic boots you can mentally put on when addressing a problem, the more ways you will have to solve it.

6. Different techniques serve different purposes. When you are stuck on a problem or can't find a creative thought to save your life, here's a technique that can help you free up your mind. Use relational prepositions to change the problem. You all know what prepositions are. They are words like: with, as, to, among, under, over, through, about, against, between, near, for, on, and, after, across, opposite. You probably can think of a lot more.

Now let's say you have a problem that relates to two major elements, i.e. *customers* and *service*. By playing with the prepositions or algorithms, you can create entirely new and creative combinations:

A. Customers *with* service implies that customers serve you as well as you serving them; they bring you valuable information about your product.

B. Customers *near* service might suggest that you need to consider bringing your service operations to locations near where your customers are.

C. Customers *under* service indicates that service could be an umbrella protecting customers – an interesting brand identification that has possibilities.

D. Customers *as* service could mean that customers provide service to other customers; a happy customer could be a great indirect salesperson.

By now you are thinking more creatively. Maybe you noticed that we could <u>reverse</u> the problem or equation altogether by putting the service first.

I. Service *over* customers suggests that you might want to place greater emphasis on service and less on sales. That way you might need less salespeople since the service will bring people back.

II. Service *before* customers might make you think about ensuring that the service needs of people are anticipated beforehand or preparations are made before the customer comes in for service.

III. Service *when* customers implies always providing service in a timely manner.

IV. Service *after* customers means ensuring that service continues after the sale and that customers know about it.

CREATIVELY RECONFIGURING THE PROBLEM

Since the problem itself is the focus of so much creative motivation and energy, one approach might be to manipulate the problem's definition. We've already seen that relational algorisms can be a useful tool when looking at the actual words in the problem. But there are other ways to make the problem work for us.

1. The first and most obvious way is to ask whether the problem can be stated differently. Once the problem is described in a different way, novel solutions might begin to appear. Portable telephones were originally viewed as emergency communication devices. They were big and clunky because they were expensive to produce. Once telephones became *chat* devices, their potential took off and, now, communication companies are finding entirely new uses for them as cameras, hand held games, and fashion accessories. *Sony Walkmans* were originally a conundrum (seemingly unsolvable problem) because they were defined as *tape recorders*. As long as the term *recorders* remained in the definition of the problem, tape machines were faulty devices. But as soon as they were viewed as *personal tape players*, their market potential became apparent.

2. Another way is to problematize's the problem definition. When the parade organizers redefined a *parade*, they were problematizing the definition of the problem by questioning whether liability or insurance needed to be involved. By focusing on situations where liability need not exist, they were able to escape from being trapped by the original formulation of the problem.

3. One of the most effective ways is to expand the problem. Sometimes alternatives to the problem cannot be found because the problem is defined too narrowly to easily permit creative solutions. You can easily expand the problem by asking: 1) what other problems are similar to this? 2) is the problem confined to one situation or is it a more general one? 3) what else can we say about this problem? 4) what are the *meanings* and *results* of this problem?

4. Similar to *problematizing the problem*, but easier, is reversing the problem. Sometimes referred to as Janusian thinking, reversing the problem means suggesting that the problem may not be a problem at all if looked at correctly. It also means highlighting opposites in the problem or its definition. A good example is *Post-It* notes. The problem with the adhesive that is now used in *Post-It* notes became a non-problem and a business success when people found out that it was useful to have an adhesive that did not stick tightly and could be peeled off easily.

Maximizing creative solutions

An important key to achieving creativity is having a diverse pool of viewpoints and perspectives from which creative solutions can be drawn. This means that individuals should get as much input from others as they can. It also means that collaboration is a terrific vehicle for achieving more creative solutions.

When you get multiple points of view aimed directly at a particular problem, you have a much better chance of finding a creative solution. That's why today's modern organizations, which operate in an environment characterized by rapid change and global competition, encourage the formation of collaborative groups or project teams. These groups can be put together, pulled apart and reconstructed so as to guarantee as much input as possible.

Individuals can create their own groups. Students find it beneficial to work together in study groups to prepare assignments. If you do form, or belong to, a group, here are a few suggestions that will help:

- Change roles in the group so that they don't become too hierarchical;

- Encourage group members to challenge solutions or play 'devil's advocate';

- Put individuals in charge of *prodding* others to achieve solutions – people tend to get lazy without prodding (it is not an enviable job; no one likes a nag; so rotate the members often!);

- Don't allow *groupthink* to happen; groupthink is when a group takes on the characteristics of an individual and becomes altogether too predictable, narrow minded, and comfortable.

ESTABLISHING A COMFORTABLE ENVIRONMENT FOR CREATIVE THINKING

Although teamwork is a potentially useful engine of creativity for the modern organization, collaboration needs to happen in a safe and comfortable environment. In the modern corporate world, teams are temporary structures. People may legitimately feel that their collaborative virtues are merely being exploited in the interest of productivity and the bottom line. In such situations, both character and creativity will inevitably suffer. People may go through the motions of being team players, but their creativity will not be empowered.

That's why establishing a more continuous and safe *environment* for creativity is so important. Recent studies of creativity suggest that some environments are more creative than others. Environments in which individuals are encouraged to take the time to relax and distance themselves a little from problems are ideal for creativity. The most difficult problems are often solved when minds are not merely allowed but encouraged to wander into unrelated areas. This loosens the hold of mental habits and allows original ideas to surface.

One of the authors of this book had the good fortune several years ago to visit a high tech software company well known for its creative products. The first thing I noticed was how relaxed the employees were. They were not *buried* in or under their work, but regularly wandered out of their cubicles to talk to each another. I was invited into the lunchroom, where my host told me to feel free to get refreshments from the fridge. The fridge contained almost every soft drink, juice and mineral water available. Employees never had to pay for their beverages. The main office included a pool table, where employees were playing pool and chatting *during their working hours*.

Obviously, not every working environment is going to be like this. But a great deal of thought went into creating this relaxed environment. Many of the characteristics of the environment were designed explicitly to break down barriers to communication and to allow employees to break out of rigid mental routines. The physical space was conducive to creative thinking, very different from either the closed offices or the isolated cubicles that characterize many corporate environments.

To the extent that you can, you want to create physical and mental environments that allow you to be creative. It is important to recognize that a relaxed environment is different from one that is too comfortable or that has too many distractions. For this reason, it's a good idea to keep the home and the working space somewhat separate or at least to differentiate functions to separate areas.

It is equally important to allow yourself reflective and recharging time when away from the workplace. One of the greatest perils to creative thinking in our society is the tendency of *passive* entertainment to push out the time needed for more *active* and *engaged* thinking. Turn off that television and the radio, unless the programs are giving you food for thought!

Don't isolate yourself away from people when you work, unless you do this in order to accomplish a particular task. Being around other people is healthy. Having a chance to talk to others about what you are reading or working on – for example, during a break – stimulates creativity. There is an important exception to this general rule. As you become more creative, interesting and informative, you will attract and be attractive to other creative people. Unfortunately, you will also find that some people will have a tendency to want to absorb your positive attributes without giving you anything in return.

It is not mean or selfish to protect yourself against toxic or negative people. Associating with negative people negates creativity. Very few people – they do exist and are wonderful – can sustain their own creativity in a negative environment.

Of course, there are even some positive environments that stifle creativity, and it's a good idea to understand them; to restrict them to their appropriate time and place; and not to allow them to intrude unduly. For example, you may enjoy going out on the town with your *buddies*. By all means, have a good time occasionally. But be aware that there may not be much creative thinking going on during these outings.

It's useful to be aware that some tensions may arise with friends and family as you grow as a person. That's why people who are very creative usually associate with others who have the same characteristics. At the end of the day, one of the best ways to become and stay creative is simply to *hang* with those who are. Just remember to always try to give as much creativity as you get!

CREATIVE BLOCKBUSTING

If you want to *bust out* of your creative *blocks*, here is a summary of the main points of this chapter.

1. The following are the primary conceptual blocks that get in the way of creative thinking:

Constancy

- · Vertical thinking

- · Verbal reasoning

- · Single cause and effect

Commitment

- · Black and white thinking

- · Stereotyping – habit and custom

- · Failing to see similarities in diverse data

Compression

- · Using narrow definition

- · Imposing rigid or artificial boundaries

- · Filtering out potentially useful information

Complacency

- · Dislike for thinking

- · Absence of curiosity

2. The following are the basic stages of creative blockbusting:

Preparation

- · Flexibility and openness

- · Expansiveness

Incubation

- · Playfulness

- · Relaxation

- · Flexibility

- · Lateral thinking

Illumination

- · Insight generation

- · Brainstorming

- · Looking for new and different relationships

Verification

- · Testing

- · Benchmarking

- · Evaluating

3. The following are a few blockbusting techniques that you might want to employ:

- · Allowing yourself to daydream

- · Following your insights and interests

- · Being patient

- Deferring judgment

- Looking at the problem from odd angles

- Reversing the problem

- Making the familiar strange and the strange familiar

- Using metaphors, analogies, symbols

- Visualizing

- Using relational algorisms

- Reading or exploring different learning materials

- Discussing issues with others

4. Finally, here are a few additional blockbusting techniques that students, as well as managers of organizations or businesses can use to free up the creative energies of employees.

  - Freeing up and tapping into motivation

  - Encouraging group collaboration; changing groups

  - Rewarding innovation and making it everyone's job

  - Defining/Recognizing creative roles

  - Judicious monitoring and prodding, not simply of production, but creative production

  - Never mistaking 'busy' work for 'productive work'

Modern society is not conducive to creative thinking. As students and employees, most of us take on way too much in the form of *busy work* and fail to build up our critical and creative reservoirs. An overly stimulated and perverse civilization of workaholics, we are rapidly losing the capacity for getting more deeply in touch with ourselves and with others. We don't burn brightly; instead, we simply burn out.

In pursuing your university and professional career, it's important to remind yourself to be self-nourishing. There is no better way of caring for yourself than developing your creativity. Unlike many aspects of life that are tedious, creativity gives our lives delight and mystery. Moreover, creativity isn't confined to a particular walk or area of life. You can creatively practice everything from cooking and needlework to painting and writing.

Some people artificially restrict the creative impulse to their hobbies or leisure activities, simply going through the motions in their jobs or university. They thereby squander a tremendous opportunity to develop and practice skills that are in short supply. If you can be creative in the way you do your work, both at school and work, you will be a far less bored and a more highly valued employee.

Look for opportunities to nurture your inner as well as outer creativity. Protect the creative child within. Give yourself time to daydream.

NOTES

[1] Donald A. Norman, *Things That Make Us Smart: Defending Human Attributes in the Age of the Machine*, (Don Mills, ON: Addison-Wesley, 1994), p. 17.

[2] Julia Cameron and Mark Bryan, *The Artists Way: A Spiritual Path to Higher Creativity*, (New York: G.P. Putnam's Sons, xi (introduction).

CHAPTER SEVEN

FINDING AND GETTING THE GREAT JOB

Keep on going and the chances are you will stumble on something, perhaps when you are least expecting it. I have never heard of anyone stumbling on something sitting down.

Charles Kettering

WHERE ARE THE JOBS?

A major problem of students about to graduate, or who have recently graduated, is knowing where the great jobs are. A good guide is to study business and political developments. If a particular industry is booming, then there likely will be many jobs to be found there, from human resources advisors to computer programmers.

Be very aware, however, that the employment marketplace is changing very fast. Don't chose a profession simply because you think there will be lots of jobs. It is far better to follow your interests and to keep both eyes open for good linkages in the workplace.

Your professors will also be a good guide to job opportunities. After all, a part of their job is to be current in their field of expertise. 12% of those who approach professors for leads are successful. But before your professor/teacher can really help you, you need to know, in your own mind, what type of job you want.

As we suggest in the previous chapters, use your years in university to help you to determine the type of employment that will give you the most satisfaction. This does not mean that you have to know exactly what you want to be, just what you like and are good at. People who decide on a career simply for economic and security reasons often have a very poor understanding of who they are and what they want out of life. If their career doesn't pan out for whatever reason they will remain adrift unless they do a lot of soul searching.

It is much easier to find a job (i.e. get work) than to discover a professional fit that is right for you. Too many people are unhappy because they are in positions that do not suit their personality. Too many people are trapped in those positions for financial and security reasons. Don't let this happen to you. Think long and hard about the kind of job that suits your temperament, and use your university experience to guide and help you in this process of self-discovery.

Don't be limited by job labels or the expectations of others. There are lots of ways to match your interests and talents with the marketplace if you take the time to make connections. The authors of this book may appear to be professional academics, but they have flexible skills. One, for example, has been at various times a University Administrator, a Placement Director for a prestigious business school, and the President of a company that liaised between governments and universities. All of these jobs were wonderful, and he wouldn't have missed out on any of them for the world.

THE IMPORTANCE OF NETWORKING

Professional organizations provide opportunities for exchanging information and ideas. But effective networking is much more than this. Networks are the informal and often invisible human relationships that govern much of what happens in the professions. No matter how bureaucratic an organization may seem, important decisions like hiring and promotion are usually based on networking. Some career experts estimate that 90% of professional appointments are never advertised. When a significant position needs to be filled, employers and managers invariably turn to those that they trust within their network.

Networks overlap and intersect with one another. Effective networking, therefore, can provide you with many potential points of contact during the course of your career. Your network can be the most important weapon you have when it comes to job hunting or promotion.

The statistics bear this out. Here are the percentages of individuals who get professional positions using various techniques (Bowles, 2002, pp. 41f)[1]:

- Internet searches or postings   4%

- Answering newspaper ads   5%

- Answering ads in the journals of your field   7%

- Mailing out tons of resumes   7%

- Going to job fairs/hiring halls   8%

- Using a government employment service   12%

- Asking a professor/teacher for job leads   12%

- Asking relatives for job leads   33%

- Applying in person to employers you   47%
  have previously researched

- Using personal contacts (networking)   86%

A particularly effective and relatively new and innovative form of networking is to form a group that works together to identify jobs and employers. That way you can share information and leads. If you are not the right person for a job, perhaps someone else in your group is and visa versa. This is a perfect strategy for recent graduates or students who are close to completing their degree. It is important to develop this joint strategy before you begin to lose contact. The overall effectiveness of this strategy is amazing; 84% of the people who work in job search groups find good jobs within a short period of time.

The sooner you start networking, the better. Most business schools encourage students to begin networking right away, on the grounds that your classmates will eventually be your business contacts. What works for business students will also work for you.

It's never too late to begin networking either. If you haven't built a network of contacts, it takes at least four months to establish a network that can help you get a professional position, even in a field where the supply exceeds the demand. These networks are fragile, however, and will collapse if not actively nurtured. It's more straightforward and natural to build a network slowly over time.

Professional networks make demands upon your talents and your time. You may find yourself helping to organize an activity, editing a journal or giving a talk. Any such professional contributions, however, will increase your skill set, as well as the size and significance of your network. Be careful to make sure your contribution is solid. The network's grapevine soon communicates the names of individuals who can be relied on and those who can't.

THE IMPORTANCE OF MAINTAINING YOUR INTEGRITY

The professional world that you seek to enter is not only a competitive marketplace but also a complex network of human relationships. At all times and places, professions have been concerned simultaneously to advance their group's interest and to preserve professional ethics and integrity. Not surprisingly, in light of the increasing consumer concern regarding the social responsibility of companies, professions are becoming even more sensitive about recruiting new members who have a strong ethical sense.

To illustrate, ethics has always played a significant role in sports and recreation. Most of those who choose careers in the field of kinesiology believe that these activities nurture important values such as sportsmanship, teamwork and respect for others. The self-discipline required to master a sport builds both cognition and character. And the emphasis on both mind and body establishes the balance without which any kind of ethical behavior would be impossible.

These ideals continue to define the discipline and the profession, despite all the recent reports of bribery, drug and sexual abuse, physical assault and hooliganism that have tarnished sports in recent years. In fact, these notorious episodes have been the catalyst for a renewal of ethical discourse and analysis in sport and the introduction of courses on ethics in the kinesiology curriculum.

Ethics, including an awareness of issues related to gender and diversity, is once again at the heart of most disciplines and it is the task of every professional to accept the responsibility they have for bringing their respective professions back into the ethical field. Undoubtedly, in the current environment, many organizations are looking for individuals who demonstrate ethical maturity and commitment. Moreover, in your professional career you should be able to demonstrate that you take your professional integrity very seriously by being able to articulate and defend your ethical values.

THE RESUME

Resumes are your professional calling card. As such, they reflect your professionalism. An effective resume implies an impressive personality. An actively worded resume implies a proactive individual – the much sought after self-starter. A well-organized resume suggests a logical and efficient person.

More nonsense has been written about resumes than almost any other subject. There is no one single model that is most effective, although many people would like to think so. A resume does not need to be confined to a single page. A two-page resume that has lots of white space may be much easier to read than a crammed single sheet. You can use coloured type in your resume, just as long as you don't overdo it.

The most important characteristic of a good resume is that it reflects the individual whose name appears on the top. The resume is a way of telling others about you. There is little sense in making your resume describe someone that is different from the real you. What purpose would that serve?

Let's say you get a job because of exaggerations or fabrications on a resume. Chances are that your employers and colleagues will soon discover that you are not the person you pretend to be. Chances are that the job you got wasn't the one that best fit your talents or interests either. Being yourself, and accurately portraying yourself, is the best way to make the best fit in the workplace.

Composing a strong resume and cover letter, however, involves more than being accurate and sincere. It requires some of the same skills as writing a strong essay. You need to be clear, concise, place yourself in the position of the reader, and so forth.

Most resume tips are just common sense:

- use a 12 pica and conservative font like Times New Roman because it is easy to read;

- highlight your education if you are a student because your education is basically you;

- highlight your work experience if you've been in the workforce a while because it reflects your professional achievements;

- include related volunteer experience because it is as important as any other work experience and also testifies to the kind of person that you are;

- use active words such as developed, achieved, earned, that emphasize achievements, rather than passive terms such as duties or responsibilities;

- only include a career objective if it applies precisely to the position advertised - why eliminate other possibilities?

- only list hobbies or interests that relate directly to the position;

- don't include references because, as a professional, it's assumed you will provide the references once an employer has decided to actively pursue you for the position;

- never have a spelling or grammatical mistake on your resume because it's one of the primary ways to eliminate applications;

- always include a cover letter that shows why you are the person who is right for the job;

- always use the highest quality (i.e. linen) paper and a laser printer because this reflects your professionalism;

- use a large sized envelope because a flat resume is much more professional (and easier to photocopy).

Professional is as professional does. Most employers are familiar with high quality printed submissions. There is zero tolerance for sloppy or poorly formatted resumes. If you don't know how to format your resume properly, pay someone who knows how to do it for you. If cost is a factor, just remember that all the time and money that you spent doing a less than perfect job is completely wasted.

Most employers and human resources professionals automatically reject all resumes:

- without a cover letter;

- with faint type or typed on a typewriter;

- containing spelling or grammar errors;

- that obviously were photocopied;

- on colored paper (except beige or gray parchment);

- on novelty paper (totally unprofessional).

The best piece of resume advice ever

You can increase you chances of a positive reaction to your resume exponentially if you provide examples of the characteristics that modern employers are looking for, such as: teamwork, problem solving, critical and creative skills, ability to work independently, multi-tasking, etc. Creative examples of how to do this effectively are provided in the samples that follow.

Resume samples

The three resumes on the next few pages provide models that you might want to consider using. Although we have changed the names, the resumes are real and were successful in getting students part-time, summer and full-time professional jobs.

The key to the success of these resumes is that considerable effort, time and thought went into each. From the perspective of a potential employer, these resumes provide the kind of information that is required to decide if the individual should be interviewed. Note how each resume is different since each person is unique, with different employment goals.

The first resume is of a student soon to graduate who has changed programs, universities, countries and employers. Yet, note how clearly this is presented.

The second resume we will look at is of a first year student. Note the choices she has made, for instance, not making reference to her high school experience. Note also the different order – with regard to education and employment – from the first resume.

The final resume illustrates how a student with limited work experience has presented her employment to-date. If she were to add information about her current post-secondary studies, her resume would be even stronger.

Hint 1 Use the table feature in your word-processing software to format your resume. Once complete, hide the borders. This will allow you to design an interesting resume, which can be easily edited.

Hint 2 Use your university e-mail address. Anyone can get a hotmail account, but not everyone is a university student. You can set up your university e-mail to automatically forward all messages to another account. Oh, and by the way, silly names like megadeath@hotmail.com send totally the wrong message to prospective employers.

Hint 3 Always highlight the position that you held, rather than your employer or place or work. Any future employer will be interested in your job, rather than the physical location where you worked.

Terry Mah

113-320 Heathdale Street, Toronto, ON M7S 6R8
voice/fax: 416-987-5678 e-mail: s.mah@yorku.ca

EDUCATION

Honors BA in History – York University, Toronto
graduating in May 2006
• specializing in 20th Century North American history
• B average overall; B+ for history courses

B.A. in the Philosophy of Religion - Beijing University, China
1998-2000 - incomplete
• majored in Buddhist philosophy

EMPLOYMENT

General Assistant - Kim and Company, Toronto
2004 - present (summer and part-time)
• Learned basic bookkeeping principles and techniques in order to support the accounting team
• Assisted clients with various inquiries on the phone and in person, while also referring more complex matters to the appropriate team member
• Maintained a clean and friendly atmosphere, including filing and ordering supplies

Front Desk Agent - Delta Chelsea Hotel, Toronto
2001-2003 (full, summer and part-time)
• Settled and confirmed guest accounts upon departure
• Assisted in the training and supervision of new staff
• Processed incoming and outgoing guests including VIPs and airline staff

Reservation Agent - Utell International, Beijing Branch
2000-2001 (full-time)
• Arranged hotel reservations worldwide, under tight deadlines
• Investigated complaints from clients and resolved these with the hotels

Researcher - China National Tourism Corporation, Beijing
1999 summer
• Conducted interviews with departing international travelers

VOLUNTEER

Student Ambassador - York University
2005 - present (3 hours/week)
• Gave prospective students and their parents tours of the university campus
• Translated from Mandarin to English for delegations visiting from China
• Directed visitors to events and provided them with information about the University

Gym teacher - St. Ann's Public School, Toronto
2004 - present (4 hours/week)
• Prepared weekly exercises for grade 4 and 5 students
• Ensured the safety of all students, including demonstrating first aid
• Arranged for students to attend Toronto Maple Leaf hockey games

Sophia Ali

Mail: 34 Hillcrest Ave, Toronto, M5A 6G6
E-mail: soph.ali@yorku.ca
Phone: 416-234-5678

Education	York University North York, Ontario	2004 - 2005

Bachelor of Arts, Business and Society
- Expected graduation, May 2008
- B+ average in first year (five courses)
- Sociology and Labor Studies stream
- University entrance scholarship recipient

**Work
Experience**   Self-employed   Toronto, Ontario   2002 – 2003
Private Tutor [evenings]

- Tutored children in grades 10 and 11 in English, French
  and mathematics
- Motivated children by organizing weekly exercises and assignments
- Responded to parent inquiries about the children's progress

Tim Horton's   Mississauga, Ontario   2001 - 2002
Assistant Supervisor [full-time]

- Learned to resolve conflicts with customers and staff
- Mainly managed energetic and inexperienced part-time staff
- Developed loyal customer relationships by memorizing the
  names and preferences of regular customers

Nortel Warehouse   Mississauga, Ontario   2000 - 2002
Returns Clerk [full-time]

- Accurately entered and retrieved product data in large
  electronic data base
- Conducted a daily physical inventory of returned products
- Packed and labeled products to prevent damage and
  ensure safe transport

**Information
Technology
Skills**
- Expert in various word-processing software
  including Word XP and WordPerfect 9.0
- Proficient in the use of spreadsheet programs,
  including Microsoft Excel and Lotus
- Superior keyboarding skills, 80 words per minute

**Other Skills and
Achievements**
- Fluent in French, reading knowledge of Hindi
- Certified group fitness (aerobics) instructor with
  teaching experience
- Volunteer experience with the developmentally handicapped

Susanna Pereira

2600 White Road, Scarborough, Ontario M3H 2M5 (416) 334-6799
Email: susan.pereira@yorku.ca

Employment

CASHIER   **Loblaws** - *16-24 hours per week*   APRIL 03-
                                                                        DECEMBER 04

- Provided friendly and patient customer service during peak times
- Managed computer operations and product knowledge
- Trained in theft control including credit card and cheque fraud

DAY CARE WORKER   **Self-employed** - *three days*   JUNE 02 -
                           a week, 8 hours per day   SEPTEMBER 03

- Cared responsibly for two children ages three and five
- Prepared nutritional and balanced meals and snacks
- Organized indoor and outdoor activities with the children

PEER LEADER (volunteer)   **Toronto Youth Outreach**   JANUARY 01 -
                           Service - *Drug and Alcohol*   JUNE 03
                           Abuse Prevention

- Conceived and developed teaching materials with other
  volunteers to be taught to grade seven and eight classes
- Motivated students by providing creative and interesting
  learning materials

TUTOR (volunteer)   **Toronto Public Library** -   MAY 2000 -
                           Homework Club   JUNE 03

- Assisted newly arrived immigrant students between the
  ages of eight and eleven with English-language homework
- Created enriched learning materials for those who finished
  their homework

THE COVER LETTER

While resumes are necessary, they are nowhere near as important as cover letters when it comes to getting you a professional position. The resume speaks to your skills, achievements and character. The cover letter tells the employer why you are the right choice for this particular position. If you think of a cover letter as a marriage proposal, you won't be very far off the mark. Employers are constantly looking for a good match between their needs and your potential contribution.

Experienced recruiters and knowledgeable employers are much more interested in your cover letter than in your resume. They'll be hoping to find clues to your personality and to discover the reasons why you chose to apply to their company or organization. They'll be flattered if they find you knowledgeable about their reputation and achievements. They'll be just as annoyed if they suspect that you are applying for positions randomly. Most of all they will have expected you to do your homework.

Do your research on the company or organization to which you are applying. Before you think about sitting down and writing a cover letter you should know as much as you can about the people you are writing to. What's the philosophy of this organization? Do they have a mission statement? What problems are they facing now? What problems will they face in the future? Your cover letter will be much more effective if it demonstrates an appreciation for the organization's achievements, culture and challenges.

Most of this basic information can be accessed on the Internet, or through annual reports. However, as a university student well versed in research and critical thinking you can add value to the information you collect. This will truly set you apart. Perhaps you have learned something from your essays you have written that applies to the company. See if you can include such information in the cover letter.

If the position has been advertised, respond directly to the wording and tone of the advertisement. Always try to show how you fit the

175

characteristics the employer is looking for. Go through them systematically in your letter. Never use a standardized letter. Always compose letters that are customized to the position. If this seems like a lot of work, just consider that the chances of getting short-listed with a standardized letter are virtually non-existent. Now that's time wasted!

Consider the tone and language of the advertisement. Does it convey dynamism? Is it precise, conservative, detailed, formal or informal? The tone and language are often the keys to understanding what kind of person an organization is looking for. Your cover letter will be more effective if it conveys the same characteristics.

Tell potential employers what you can do for them. Students' cover letters are typically full of the things that an organization can provide, but very thin about how they are going to contribute to the company. Corporate recruiters routinely weed out those kinds of submissions, looking for candidates who are self-starters and proactive problem solvers with up-to-date knowledge acquired from their university courses.

Take great care with the construction of your cover letter. The number of resumes that are thrown out because students write clumsy and ungrammatical cover letters would astonish you. More than one spelling mistake in a cover letter or resume typically means that it goes straight into the wastebasket!

Don't try to be someone that you are not. Look for companies that are looking for people with your characteristics. Even if you successfully use the techniques mentioned above to land a job, you won't be happy unless the fit is genuine.

Cover letter sample

There is a basic format to most cover letters (as there is to all documents, be they essays or poems). Below is the format you are most likely to use. However, again, the purpose of the cover letter is to reveal something about you that will help the potential employer make a decision. As such, do not feel bound to follow it slavishly; rather adapt it to fit your particular circumstances.

A. The introductory paragraph is where you state your interest in the position and try to capture your reader's attention. The language here needs to convey genuine interest without being unprofessional. The hook for the reader is often company specific knowledge or a compliment (genuine, not flattery).

A typical opening might be:

"I read with interest your advertisement for a vacancy in physical therapy at St. Joseph's Hospital. The quality of healthcare at St. Joseph's is exceptional and it would be a privilege to join your physical therapy team."

B. The first paragraph following the introduction is where you state your strengths and the added value that you can bring to the organization.

"As a recent graduate of York University's Kinesiology and Health Science Program, I am familiar with the very latest theoretical and practical approaches in the field. Not only do I have the expertise in athletic injuries that your organization seeks, but also I have four years experience working as an intern at several university sports clinics. My supervisors rated my work as 'supremely professional' and my clinical skills as close to matching those 'who have worked in the profession for many more years than she has'."

C. The next paragraph allows you to provide a more detailed summary of your relevant education and experience. This is the place where you might identify the specific courses you have taken, particulars of your internships, and any special attributes that might help sell you to a potential employer.

D. If necessary, you can add a short paragraph that explains any problems that the employer is likely to spot. For example, you need to be proactive about any gaps in your career.

E. If possible, you should try to add a paragraph that will help to solve any problems that an organization or the related industry is facing. This is a good way to introduce some new knowledge or techniques that you have learned at university.

F. A sentence or two that describes the follow up action that you are going to take. You need to demonstrate that you are proactive and are not going to passively wait for a call from the employer.

"I look forward to an opportunity to discuss the position and my contributions in greater detail through a personal interview. I will call next Tuesday to determine your interest and to arrange an appointment."

G. A sentence that shows appreciation for being considered for the employment position. This is a formal thank you that can take a number of forms.

"Thank you for considering my application. I wish you every success in filling this important position."

Things you should avoid

Blandness: You need to capture your reader's attention; you can't achieve that if you compose bland and boring prose.

Rambling: You need to focus on the job and the match between an employer's needs and your credentials. You can, and should, inject a bit of your personality, but you certainly don't need to tell them everything about yourself.

Excessive self-focus: You have to talk about yourself in a cover letter, but your overriding focus should always be the employer or organization to which you are applying.

Bad grammar, style, and punctuation: It should be obvious that these are the kiss of death for any serious application. Every bit of work you put into your application will be wasted if you don't get this right.

Conceit: There is a fine line between understanding your potential worth to an organization and engaging in bragging. Again, if you focus on the employer's needs, you will avoid the egocentricity that leads to bragging.

Self-deprecation: A faint heart never won fair bride. If ever there was a time to be assertive about what you have to offer an organization, it's in your cover letter and your interview. Everyone understands that this is a time to sell yourself. Timidity is not the characteristic of a good problem solver.

Aggression: Students either seem to lack assertiveness altogether or to go to the other extreme. Pushiness is rarely effective. Don't tell a potential employer what he or she should do. Don't give them dates that you will be available for an interview.

Length: One page letters are best. It's o.k. to spill over to a second page if your letter is well written, but never fill that second page.

Here is a sample cover letter. As the employer, would you call the applicant for an interview, based on this submission?

Cover letter sample

Andre Highbutt
Any Street
Toronto, ON L7S 2A5

Phone: 416-xxx-xxx
E-mail: my.name@yorku.ca

July 27, 2005

Department of Human Resources
York University

Attention: Recruiting Officer

Dear Sir/Madam,

I read with interest your advertisement for a part-time Reserve Assistant in Scott Library Circulation Department. If you need someone with superior organizational skills, and an ability to communicate concisely with different kinds of people in complex situations, I would like the opportunity to talk to you.

The attached resume describes someone who has studied at York University for two years and who has a keen interest in working with diverse communities and providing help to students and faculty. It highlights the attention to detail, quality control and processing skills that are included in your major areas of responsibility. And, hopefully, it describes someone that you would like to have working with you and ensuring that your services are provided in an efficient and timely manner.

Although I have no experience working in a university library, I have considerable experience in the book industry. In my current employment position, I have the responsibility for purchasing and selling books. Last year, I volunteered my services for three months to the Mobile City Library, an innovative library lending service in a neighborhood mall.

I hope that my skills and experience will be of interest to you as you seek someone to fill the position. I look forward to hearing from you and talking to you about the ways that I could contribute to the functioning of a library that I have long used and enjoyed.

I trust you will not mind if I call early next week to follow up on the status of my application and, hopefully, to set up a time, at your convenience, to discuss the position.

Thank you for considering my resume. I look forward to hearing from you.

Sincerely yours,

Patrick Highbutt

resume attached

THE INFORMATIONAL INTERVIEW

Don't let the number of books and businesses devoted to resumes and cover letters mislead you about the most important aspect of the job search. Networking is more effective than formally applying for advertised jobs, even if you have the world's greatest resume or cover letter. But what if you've spent most of your waking hours either studying or working at a part-time job and have absolutely zero networking experience? Where do you begin?

Fortunately, there's a well-established and universally understood mechanism for networking called the informational interview. An informational interview is a brief question and answer session with someone who works in a profession or for a company that interests you.

The someone in question is not an employer, or a person who has the power to hire you. They are individuals who enjoy their work and are willing to spend a few minutes talking to you about it. The whole idea behind an informational interview is that there is no pressure and lots of shared enthusiasm. It is also the place where you begin to add people to your network.

It is relatively easy to arrange an informational interview. Most professionals are familiar with them and are willing to share information about the work they enjoy. Your professors will probably know a number of graduates working in the field you are interested in and be able to give you at least one name. Once you have their name, you give that person a call and ask for ten minutes of their time at their convenience. Let them know that it is just information about their work that you are interested in, so that they know there are no strings attached. Assure them that you will take no more than ten minutes of their time, because in today's world all professionals feel the pressure of too many things to do and not enough minutes in the day.

You will need to purchase some 3 x 5 index cards, an alphabetical index and a container to keep the names, addresses and comments on your contacts. You will also need to purchase some thank you notes.

The ones that spell out Thank You are more appropriate for domestic than professional use. Professional looking cards with art scenes that are blank on the inside are ideal for your networking purposes.

Dress appropriately. This is an informal interview, so you probably don't have to wear a suit, tie or the other trappings of a formal interview. Take your cue from the way that professionals in the field dress when they go to work. If in doubt, lean towards more rather than less dressy.

Some people feel that they cannot be themselves in formal attire. That is a very foolish and self-defeating attitude. Most professions have a dress code, even if it involves a range of choices. Those who work in professions are not any less unique individuals because they conform to an accepted standard.

Arrive early. This sends the message that you respect the time of your interviewee. Stick strictly to the 10-minute schedule.

Questions to ask at informational interviews

· Why did you choose your profession?

· How did you get your first job after graduating from university?

· What do you like most about your work?

· What do you like least about your work?

· If you only had one piece of advice to give someone who was considering entering your profession, what would it be?

· Can you give me the name/names and phone numbers of other people I might talk to about the profession?

· Can I use your name when I contact them?

· Can I get the correct spelling of your name and address so that I can send you a thank you note?

After the Informational Interview

The first task after an informational interview is to thank the person for giving you some of their valuable time. When you get home, put the interviewee's name on a 3 x 5 inch index card, or create a computer file, with a couple of comments about the session. While the interview is still fresh in your head, compose and send a thank you note to your interviewee.

Begin building your network. By following up on the leads given to you by your interviewee, you will soon build up a file of index cards of possible contacts in the profession. Always follow up with all the names that you have been given. Like all human relationships, you will click with some people more than others, and feel comfortable contacting them again. Congratulations! You've begun to build a network.

Keep your network warm. Be careful not to bother your contacts unnecessarily. But don't hesitate to drop them a note letting them know how your interviews went with the people they recommended. Because professional networks are complex and overlapping, you will continually run into people who know others that you have interviewed. This gives you another opportunity to drop a note. Some of your contacts will use your visit as an opportunity to call or renew contact with someone else on your list. Over time, your name becomes known and your interest in the profession becomes documented.

Use your network strategically. If a job opportunity arises check your network file to:

- inquire if you have any contacts in the organization that has the vacancy;

- ask your contacts whether they think the position is suitable for a person like you;

- seek advice on how best to apply for the position;

· see if you can find out what are the major issues or problems facing the organization;

· identify the person that is actually responsible for the hiring, and whether or not it would be appropriate to contact them directly. Personally contacting the person responsible for the hiring, rather than simply entering the hiring process, greatly multiplies your chance of success.

Timetable

Don't expect a fully functional network to appear overnight. Unless you have an inside track, it usually takes several months for a network to begin to produce fruit in terms of tips and opportunities. People who decide to change careers report that it takes approximately 4-6 months to build a workable network in the new field.

The best possible practice is to start your network while in university. Ask your professors or TAs for names of people (former students, etc.). Attend seminars or workshops on topics of interest and try to get to know the speakers. If you have guest speakers in your classes, speak to them for a minute or two after their talk. Get their business card. Contact them later. They might not remember you, but they will be pleased that a student remembers them and wants more information.

If you are conducting research for an essay or presentation you have an ideal opportunity to make contacts and obtain information. Courses with a placement component are an excellent means to create a network. To wait to build your network until you start looking for a job wastes the opportunities you have to network while in school. Moreover, if you start early and keep your network warm over a period of years rather than months, it will be a more genuine, hence effective, relationship.

A creative way to energize your network

Toronto *Metro* education and workplace columnist, Jill Andrew offers this useful tip for those engaged in networking. Consider composing a short 3 – 500 word article on "something interesting or a *hot topic* that relates either to your academic life or extracurricular interests." If you can "relate your academic and extracurricular activities to a desirable field of work, all the better."

A well-written article will: 1) get you noticed; 2) provide you with a legitimate excuse for *warming* your network; and 3) give you a document to leave with interviewees and interviewers. Consider including quotes from professors or professional in your network, since these "always help to validate any story and make it more newsworthy."

Local newspapers are always looking for new and timely material (especially if it's free!). If you think the article is good enough, why not submit it to a larger daily or electronic news wire. What have you got to lose?

Misuse of informational interviews

Every good thing is subject to abuse. In recent years, some individuals have begun to use informational interviews disingenuously as job-hunting mechanisms. Employers and professionals resent being used in this way. It is critical, therefore, that you are honestly seeking information about a professional career that you are genuinely interested in. It is equally important that you do not use the informational interview as a way of getting others to do your job search for you. Finally, never use the informational interview as a deceitful way of getting in to see someone that you hope will give you a job.

THE REAL INTERVIEW

In *What Color is Your Parachute*, the best of all the job hunting books, Richard Bolles estimates that 98% of applicants go into job interviews like sheep to the slaughter. The sheep are all those who fail to understand that interviews are all about sizing one another up in order to see if there is a good match.

This sizing up process is a lot like dating. You should be yourself, but be yourself on your very best behavior. You wouldn't reveal everything about yourself on a first date, would you? You'd be advised to listen as much as talk, wouldn't you? You'd want to do things to ensure that your first date wasn't your last I hope. The same is true of an interview.

There exist a set of conventions about interviews that you should be aware of. These include:

- Wearing formal attire. It doesn't matter what makes you comfortable. The interviewer expects you to dress formally for a professional interview.

- You should be approximately ten minutes early. This indicates that you have given yourself lots of time to get to the interview and that you respect the time of the other person.

- You may be asked whether you would like a cup of coffee. The right answer is "No, thank you." It's not professional to be sipping coffee while you are being interviewed.

- Trained interviewers may begin by making light conversation to make you feel comfortable. Understand this for what it is, and don't be tempted to relax. Be aware that a complex interaction is about to happen. Again, think of a date and you won't be far off.

- Most interview questions have a hidden meaning. These will be discussed a little further on. But many of them are probing for problems in your past or your personality that might make you unsuitable.

· The interviewer is always looking for signs that you may be 1) unmotivated 2) lazy 3) unenthusiastic 4) arrogant 5) irresponsible 6) whiny 7) uncollegial 8) indiscreet or unethical, or 9) have problems with authority. Therefore, it is important that you are careful to monitor your responses to ensure that you don't send any signals of these problematic behaviors.

On the positive side, the employer is looking for signs that you will fit in and that you have the ability to learn new skills and apply those you have acquired at university. This implies that the more information you provide that demonstrates maturity, responsibility, collegiality, and the communication and critical skills honed at university, the better.

You are expected to make good eye contact and it's advisable to smile. It is not a good idea to joke, to be ironic, to be sarcastic, to be witty or any of the things that might detract from your professionalism. Many of those behaviors signal a potentially problematic personality.

Bring copies of some of your work to the interview including essays you are proud of, your transcript, and other documents from school or your past/current job. You may not always need these, but they give you a sense of confidence that you can provide tangible evidence of your accomplishments. If you are not asked for these, you can still – if appropriate – offer to leave a copy behind. Doing so will differentiate you from other applicants and give those who will decide on whom to hire something to remember you by.

You will be asked whether or not you have questions for them. If you don't, you've squandered a real opportunity to indicate knowledge and interest in their organization. You've probably also left the impression that you're too passive and needy.

Your self-composure, intelligence and professionalism are always being tested, whether or not it is evident. Some interviews are grilling sessions; some seem to be a walk in the park. Don't be misled by this. Keep your composure and a positive attitude, even if you think your interviewer hates you. You might be pleasantly surprised.

By the same token, just because your interview was a pleasant experience, it doesn't mean that you are a shoo-in for the position. Be realistic. Just because your first date went well, it doesn't mean that you're going to get a marriage proposal.

You can learn a lot from those two very popular television programs, *The Bachelor* and *The Bachelorette*. The nicest person or the one that you think is the most handsome/beautiful doesn't always win the prize. Sometimes the prize isn't even worth the effort, as some successful candidates discovered afterwards. At the same time, it's easy to spot people who screw up in the dating game by giving too much away too early, by being too needy, or by sending signals that they just might belong in a psycho ward!

Interviews usually end abruptly. Interviewers are usually on a tight schedule. You may feel dismissed when the interview comes to an abrupt end. When the interviewer concludes the session, it's a very important time to retain your composure, rise quickly, shake the hand of your interviewer and thank him/her/them for the interview courteously, and leave. Don't try to throw in any last comments, or to say how much you like their organization, or whatever. It's over; get out of there!

All things being equal, those who send a thank you note after the interview have a much better chance of getting the position than those who don't. Moreover, if there was something you wanted to add at the end of the interview, this is the right place to do it.

Exceptions

There are exceptions to every rule, of course. Some of your interviewers may not follow these rituals at all. They may decide to hire you precisely because you were sarcastic, wore sneakers to the interview, or displayed an aggressive personality. But don't bet on it. The message you send by not adhering to the rules is that you might be a problem. The last thing today's organization wants is a potential problem.

Think about it. It costs an organization approximately five thousand dollars to recruit a professional. It costs them many times that much to get rid of a person who doesn't fit in. Today's employer does not have the same access to personal information about candidates as the employer of the past. He or she cannot get rid of a poor employee as easily as in the past either. For this reason, the modern employer almost always tries to play it safe when selecting a person for a professional position.

In general, regardless of the interview situation, it is best to err on the side of conservatism. Don't offer interviewers your full personality. The interview is neither the time nor the place for full disclosure.

THE THANK YOU LETTER

A thank you letter should never be more than a page long. It's usually never read, but that doesn't make it any less effective. What will be remembered is that you took the time to write and send it. Read on for a sample thank you letter.

Thank you letter sample

Bryan Someone
24 Homewood Ave
Markham, ON L4S 2Y1

Phone: xxx-xxx-xxxx
email: Brian.some@internet.com

April 15, 2005

Sabrina Makhamra
Summer Programs Manager
Happy Summer Camps
Orillia, Ontario XXX XXX

Dear Ms. Makhamra:

It was a delight to meet you yesterday and learn more about Happy Summer Camps. I appreciate the time you spent showing me the impressive camp facilities and reviewing the responsibilities of the summer coordinator position.

During our conversation, you stressed the important role that the summer coordinator has in training the counselors. You may be assured that my education program at university and previous summer camp positions, specifically as assistant staff supervisor last summer at Lakeview Camp, have prepared me for the coordinator position.

Thank you once again for your time and consideration. I'm excited about the possibility of making this summer the best one ever for both the staff and children at Happy Summer Camps.

I look forward to hearing from you.

Sincerely,

Bryan Someone

DECODING INTERVIEW QUESTIONS

As with answering essay questions on exams, the key to a successful interview is to understand the question. Below we decode many of the questions that you will be asked during an interview.

A. Tell me about yourself

translation: Here's some rope. Want to hang yourself?

explanation: This question suggests that you are not dealing with an experienced interviewer. An inexperienced interviewer feels more in control if you are doing all the talking and they can sit back and spot the weaknesses. An experienced interviewer prefers to probe directly and not to waste time with such an open-ended approach. It is impossible to assess someone's personality in a short interview. The person who asks this question, therefore, is looking for potential problems that you might bring with you.

solution: Your task is to briefly suggest that you are a reliable person with a good employment track record who has profited from being in university, not to blurt out your life. You can answer this question constructively by quoting some good things that your employers, teachers or references say about you. Be courteous even though this is an unprofessional question.

duration: Two minutes tops. It's not a serious or appropriate question.

B. Why did you apply for this job?

variation: What kind of work are you looking for?

translation: I want you to show us how you fit our precise needs.

explanation: Obviously your interviewer knows a lot more about what the organization is really looking for in this job than you do. The question is an attempt to get you to narrow down what you want out of the position before you know the details. Then if you don't fit, they can eliminate you.

solution: If you know exactly what they are looking for (i.e. through your contacts, your study of the organization) show them how you are precisely the person they need. If not, turn the question around and ask them for more details about the kind of job that's involved. Say something like, "I'd love to talk about my suitability for the position, but perhaps you could give me some more information about what the position specifically involves so that I can see whether or not there's a good match between my skills and your needs."

duration: Up to 10 minutes. This is the heart of the issue.

C. What experience/expertise do you have in this line of work?

variation: What makes you think you'd be good at this job?

translation: You probably can't do this job. You don't have the exact experience needed.

explanation: This is the question most often directed at those who are entering the professional marketplace and don't yet have the experience that many employers want to demand.

solution: Don't apologize for your lack of experience or tell them how willing you are to learn. That will only make you look needy. What you want to do here is to show how your education has provided you with the state-of-art knowledge that can be applied to the position. You also want to argue that you have transferable skills, including your professionalism that can be applied to the position. Finally, you want to remind them that you've mastered many things in the past and will do so in the future.

duration: Up to ten minutes. This is where you "sell yourself."

D. Can you provide us with an example of a difficult situation that you were in with people in the past and how you handled it?

variation: How did you get along with previous employers or co-workers?

translation: Prove to us that you are not difficult to get along with.

explanation: Modern organizations are based on collaboration and teamwork. It is far more important, especially for an entry-level position, to have an employee that can work with others than even the most brilliant leader who is hard to get along with. If there is any evidence at all that you could be a difficult person, you will not get the job.

This question can have several layers that become more apparent in the discussion. One of the areas that the interviewer will be probing is whether you have a tendency to criticize your employers or fellow workers. If you are prone to do this, it is the kiss of death. If you do this in an interview, when you are on your best behavior, chances are that you will do it even more frequently on the job.

The interviewer may try to push you into discussing a situation where you had a serious conflict with an employer, co-worker or teacher. Since almost everyone who has ever breathed on the planet will have at least one bad working relationship, you cannot avoid this trap.

solution: Provide the interviewer with an employment situation where you acted maturely in order to get people on your side or to resolve conflicts. Try to find ways to say nice things about your past employers and co-workers. Always emphasize the strong qualities that you demonstrated in conflicts and the positives that you took from difficult people and situations.

If a skillful interviewer probes for a real conflict, don't hesitate to give them one. Just remember to deal with it maturely and as a learning experience. Be careful not to `bad mouth' even the most irritating behavior. Your purpose in the interview is to show that you are above any pettiness, even if you clearly have been wronged. Haven't we all? It's how we deal with it that counts.

duration: This can take anywhere from 10 to 15 minutes depending on the depth of probing.

E. Can you explain the gap in your work-school history?

variations: Why did you take a year out between high school and university? Why did it take you five years to complete a four-year program? What were you doing during this particular year that is missing from your resume?

translation: Are you a quitter, a failure or a slacker?

explanation: Employment gaps used to be the biggest black spots on an employee's resume. In the modern marketplace, employers expect more transitions and view change more positively than in earlier decades. But gaps still provide an opportunity to probe.

solution: Your job is to show them that you are really dedicated to your work. It is because you take what you do so seriously that you took extra time out to get prepared for the challenge or to renew your skills. You want to show what you did during these gaps that will make you a better person or a better employee. You also want to reassure them that you are making a serious (i.e. at least a five-year) commitment to them.

duration: Five minutes tops.

F. Tell us about a problem that you solved in life, school or work

variation: Have you ever experienced a serious problem in your life? How did you solve it?

translation: Prove to us that you are a problem solver.

explanation: This is a positive question. It is an attempt to discover if you have the critical skills that we have been exploring throughout this book. In the modern global environment, employers are looking for people who can identify problems before they become bigger problems and discover creative solutions.

One of the biggest problems faced by modern employers is the passive employee who does a fair job of the tasks that he or she is given, but who does not otherwise contribute to the survival and success of the organization. To simultaneously discover a person who will solve problems while not adding to an organization's existing problems is the goal of every good interviewer.

solution: It is impossible to give a good answer to this question unless you have developed your critical skills. Contrived answers are pretty easy for an experienced interviewer to spot, and further probing will only expose more fundamental weaknesses. At the same time, a good answer to this question requires preparation. You need to think about issues in your past or at work and how you have handled them. If you haven't handled them as well as you might have liked, say so, and discuss how you would handle those same problems today.

What you really want to do is to show that you know how to identify a problem and work logically to a solution. You also want to show that you are a lateral, as well as a vertical, thinker who can apply creative solutions to problems. Finally, you want to show that some of the most creative solutions to problems come from working collaboratively with others. If you are able to bring creativity and collaboration together with problem solving, you will make a good impression on your interviewer.

You can use examples from your studies in replying to this (and other questions). Perhaps, you got stuck in a group project with someone who failed to contribute. How did you handle this problem? How would you handle a similar problem in the workplace?

duration: Up to ten minutes.

G. What is your greatest weakness?

variation: What personal qualities do you feel you need to work on to be a better person or employee?

translation: Tell us what's wrong with you so that we can reject you immediately.

explanation: With experienced interviewers, this comes near the end, when you are getting just a bit tired or cocky. It's a serious trap designed with no other purpose in mind than to eliminate you as a candidate. It is the question from hell, if you are not prepared for it.

Honest, but inexperienced candidates often get lured in by this question, especially if they feel that the interview is going well and they have a good feeling about the interviewer. It doesn't matter how nice the interviewer is, this question is part of the standard repertoire and its purpose is to identify a weakness. Uninformed honesty is not the best policy for dealing with this question.

solution: The good thing is that everyone has weaknesses. You are not in the confessional. You don't have to tell a priest your sins. Give them a weakness that is also a strength. "I have a tendency to work a little too hard when I'm completing an interesting project," is the kind of weakness that never lost anyone a job. You can even make a weakness work for you. "I'm a person that likes to take the initiative and to always do more than is expected. This means that I occasionally get irritated if I'm being supervised too closely." If you get the job, your supervisor will probably be told to give you more freedom than usual.

duration: Five minutes tops, unless you can turn this into a discussion of your ideal working environment.

H. Where do you expect to be in your career in five years time?

variation: How do you want your career to develop?

translation: Are you just looking for a paycheck or a meaningful career?

explanation: Employers want to know whether or not you are a good investment. Are you the kind of person who could grow with the organization and fulfill successively responsible positions in the firm? That would be their ideal.

The five-year specification is a meaningful one. In many professions, it's expected that people may jump to other organizations after five years in order to advance their careers. Sometimes it's easier to advance by moving than by staying in the same place. You need to be aware of this, if only because they are aware of it.

Your parents probably didn't get this question or its variations in an interview. During the 1950s and 1960s, most employers expected people to stay with the same organization most of their lives. They were looking for candidates who would be responsible and predictable in carrying out well-defined duties. The world has changed and today's employers want much more proactive workers. But those in charge of organizations do want to think that they can hold on to their most valuable employees by providing them with opportunities for promotion within the firm.

solution: You need to show that you are reasonably ambitious, which means you need to have done some research on your career and its probable trajectory. You want to tell the employer that you are the kind of person who thrives on challenges and opportunities, without looking as though you are going to shake up their organization overnight. You want to look like someone who will grow and develop in your career.

In five years you want to have developed your professional skills to the point where your employers would recognize your growth and place you in appropriate positions. The implication can be that you would seek those challenges elsewhere if they were not forthcoming from your organization. But you should never explicitly say this or your commitment might come into question.

duration: Up to five minutes.

I. What are your salary expectations?

variation: What was your salary in your previous job?

translation: Can we afford you?

explanation: Your potential cost is always on the employer's mind in the interview, especially if you are an impressive candidate with specialized degrees and experience. Employers know that questions about salary are unprofessional at this stage of the proceedings, but they often don't care if they can get information that will help them decide between equally good candidates.

Also, employers know that you are in a much better bargaining position once you have been offered the job. You make their life easier if you fall into the trap of agreeing to salary numbers prior to them committing.

solution: You never know what kind of pressure an employer/interviewer is going to put on you in an interview. For this reason, it's always a good idea to have a salary range in mind that you've arrived at by looking at the statistical averages for your profession. But it is important not to negotiate salary unless your hand is forced.

Simply suggest that it isn't your practice to discuss remuneration unless a formal offer of employment has been made and you are seriously considering taking a position. You prefer to concentrate on the issue at hand, which is to discover whether or not there is a good match between your skills and their needs.

If you are offered a job, you enter into the salary negotiation at that time. Once they've decided on you, they will not want to start interviewing for the position again. You will be able to leverage the highest salary possible at that time. Be prepared to be reasonable, but also remember that it is much easier to get higher remuneration when you are hired than after you are in place.

duration: Under normal conditions this question should be dealt with in less than a minute, since you do not want to commit at this time.

J. Do you have any questions for us?

variation: Is there anything that you'd like to ask us?

translation: This is your opportunity to size us up.

explanation: Most of the interview is structured around their questions and your responses. A skillful candidate will have a set of questions in mind for the interviewer before beginning the interview and will ask these where appropriate. The rule of thumb for a good interview is that the interviewer and the interviewee each talk for fifty per cent of the time. This is a clear sign of matchmaking, where two individuals are feeling each other out and engaging in a courtship ritual.

Depending on the nature of the interview, this may not be possible. Especially when there are a large number of candidates for a position, or when there is more than one interviewer, the candidate's questions may be left to the end of the interview.

Even if the interviewers are not particularly interested in the candidate's questions, they will expect the candidate to have some. Not to have questions implies either: 1) neediness, 2) lack of interest, or 3) insufficient research on the position and the organization.

solution: You should have some questions about the position or the organization that demonstrate that you have done your homework. It's always very effective to highlight one of the issues or problems that the organization, industry or profession is facing and to seek your interviewers' opinion. Make the most of this opportunity to demonstrate your knowledge and interest.

Your interest and involvement should not be self-absorbed. It's fine to ask for clarification of some aspects of the position or to elaborate on an earlier answer, but the most effective use of this time is to demonstrate your interest in them rather than your needs or desires. That's the approach that's most effective in dating and in job hunting.

duration: Variable, but prepare a good 10 minutes worth of questions, even if the responses are abbreviated. We give you ten questions to ask below.

Questions to ask at the formal interview

1. Can you describe a typical day on the job?

2. What are your organization's three top goals during the coming year?

3. What are the biggest challenges in this position?

4. What are the major challenges facing your organization?

5. What are the career opportunities for someone who excels in this position?

6. What is your organization's management style or philosophy?

7. How do you rank this position in terms of the organization's bottom line?

8. What kinds of people succeed best in this organization?

9. What kinds of people have not succeeded in this organization?

10. What is your ideal employee?

On campus services and interviews

Your university probably has a career preparation office. You would be wise to visit it and see what information and services are available that might help you. You may find much or little, but it is crucial to check. However, at the end of the day finding the ideal job for you is largely a do-it-yourself project.

Some employers conduct on-campus interviews that tend to be coordinated by the career services/placement office. Signing up for these can be a good opportunity to prepare your resume and, if offered an interview, practice your interview skills.

Interviews at small companies

A great deal of the advice provided above is tailored to large organizations with trained human resources personnel. Many new jobs being created these days, however, are with small companies where the employer is also the interviewer. This development has its pros and cons for the job hunter.

On the positive side, the person with the actual power to give you a job will probably interview you. On the other hand, it is unlikely that this individual will have been trained in interviewing. Human resources professionals have considerable expertise at putting people at their ease and structuring the interview process in such a way as to discover a candidate's potential.

Untrained interviewers are often nervous and uncomfortable when screening candidates. They can also be insensitive, and occasionally offensive, even if that is not their intention. In these situations, many of the rituals outlined above are superfluous and your strategy should change accordingly.

Here's what you need to remember if the owner of a small company or organization is interviewing you:

· He/she is probably just as nervous as you are;

· You have the responsibility for ensuring that the right questions get asked;

· Putting the interviewer at ease with you is critical;

· Follow-up after the interview is even more critical, since the nterviewer is unlikely to have a good basis for making a decision;

· Don't be hard on yourself if you don't get the job. The interview was good practice and there will be many more opportunities if you are scouting small companies;

· Try to add the employer to your network. There's a good chance that they made the wrong decision and may be looking for someone in the future.

In many respects, small companies are the ideal environments for personal growth because they are less bureaucratic and provide many more opportunities to develop your professional skills.

The smaller companies cannot invest as heavily in recruitment and, therefore, rely more on networking to find employees. Smaller companies are also much more likely to entertain non-traditional working relationships.

One of the most effective ways to break into the small company marketplace is to offer to work for free for a limited period of time in order to gain professional experience. Larger organizations rarely entertain these kinds of relationships because: 1) their human resources departments disapprove of such irregular hiring; and 2) issues of company liability usually get raised within the bureaucracy. Small companies will often try people out with contracts or part-time positions. For them, it's an excellent way to see whether someone fits in without having to go through a tedious process of recruitment and dismissal.

Overall, therefore, you should be thinking about the opportunities being created by small innovative businesses. For people who are just starting out, these companies may be the best places to break in and obtain professional experience.

INTERVIEW STYLES

Interviewing techniques change all the time. Although the interview tips we have provided here will work for you nine times out of ten, you should be aware that some organizations have opted for very different ways of conducting an interview.

The conversational approach

Here, the interviewer engages the candidate in conversation rather than asking direct questions. The probing is done in such a relaxed and casual manner that it is easy for the candidate to be caught off guard and to reveal too much information. The key here is to remember the rules for performing well in an interview and never to let down your professional guard.

The consensus approach

Because of the significant cost of recruiting and retaining good employees, many organizations have developed a team approach to interviewing, on the grounds that several heads are better than one when it comes to choosing a prospective employee. These interviews can be daunting because the candidate needs to deal with several different, and sometimes conflicting, personalities.

It's obviously impossible to control the variables in these situations as well as in a one-on-one interview. The secret here is to practice good listening skills so that you can pick up on the sub-texts of the questions of individuals while maintaining good eye contact and rapport with the entire team. Taking time answering questions is the most important thing you can do here. If someone suspects that you are nervous and tries to help you, just gently inform them that you are thinking about the best way to address the question.

Although consensus interviews can seem stressful, they are actually a lot easier to perform well in than the one-on-one with a skillful interviewer. The probing is far less deep and the differences among the team give you lots more time to pay attention to the dynamics.

The stress approach

A new kind of interview technique is to put the candidate under stress. This is often accomplished by a variety of boorish techniques, including: 1) making highly controversial statements with a demand for your immediate response; 2) responding to your questions or answers with prolonged silence.

The effectiveness of this approach is highly questionable. The assumption being made is that the modern world is a stressful place and the best employees are those that can deal with anxiety. There might be some validity in this, were it not for the fact that the stress interview is a relatively easy one to master. The strategy for coping is to: 1) keep your cool; 2) calmly deflect uncomfortable questions; and 3) diffuse controversial statements by reinterpreting them in a professional manner; 4) always aim for a balanced and judicious response, despite the tone or aggression of the interviewers.

Since the whole point of a stress interview is to see if you will break under pressure, all you have to do is stay calm.

All day and restaurant interviews

Many of today's professional organizations like to spend an entire day or at least an extended meal with the candidate. The idea here is that, while a person may be able to hide aspects of his or her personality during a short interview, the real character comes out in the course of a busy day or an evening meal. That's debatable, but, if this happens to you, there are some things that you need to be aware of.

Your stomach is potentially your worst enemy during these extended negotiations. Mealtimes may be different from what you are used to, and you need to keep the blood flowing to your brain rather than your tummy. Some of the best pieces of advice for these events are: 1) to carry a plentiful supply of nutritious snacks in case you get hungry; 2) to give alcohol and red meats a pass at mealtime. The only good thing about these kinds of interviews is that you are not expected to pay for the food.

The second and third interview

One of the signs of just how seriously large organizations now take the hiring process is the evolution of successive interviews. It used to be that one interview was enough. These days, sometimes three interviews are insufficient and hopeful candidates may find themselves going through a roller-coaster ride of interviews that may take many weeks and even several months.

This provides you with some very good reasons for relaxing about the interview process. It isn't healthy to get too worked up about a position that you might have to interview for several times with different people. The time between the first and third interviews is the right time to reflect on the nature of the organization and whether it's really the right place for you. A little self-induced doubt is a handy attitude to take into these interviews because it will translate as greater independence.

Experienced job hunters never put all their eggs in one basket. They always apply for several jobs around the same time. That way, if you are not successful, you can immediately turn your thoughts to other opportunities rather than brooding about the one that got away.

REFERENCES

You may be asked for your references at the interview or shortly thereafter if you are being seriously considered. In most occupations it is uncommon, and even unprofessional, to be asked for references when you apply for a position.

Sometimes your references may be asked to provide letters that are attached to your application, but most times the potential employer will only contact references if you are being seriously considered.

Choosing references carefully is critical, because potential employers place significant value on what your references have to report about you. With one exception, discussed below, never give someone's name as a reference unless you have asked first. Also, explain the type of job that you are applying for. Be sure to make certain that the person you ask is comfortable in the role of referee; if not, find someone else.

Giving the name of your current employer as a reference can raise complex issues (disloyalty, for example). One approach is to provide your current employer as a reference, but with a request that he/she only be contacted if you are very seriously under consideration and that you be told first. This allows you to speak to your current employer only when he/she is going to be contacted.

Professors tend generally to be good references, since they are perceived to be impartial. If there is a professor or two that you click with, do not hesitate to ask. However, remember that sometimes (i.e. in the summer) professors can be away on research trips and unable to respond to requests for references.

Typically you will be asked to provide three references. Aim for a mix: your current employer, a professor, a past employer, someone with whom you have done volunteer work and so forth.

Your three references should be typed on a piece of paper in something like the format shown on the next page. You want to provide the full information about how your contacts can be reached and to have your list ready when asked for (such as with you during an interview). As we illustrate on the reference format, it is acceptable to include very short notes on the referees to make it as easy as possible for these to be identified and reached.

References sample

References for [insert your name]

Prof. Thomas Klassen
Department of Political Science
Faculty of Arts
York University
4700 Keele Street
Toronto, Ontario M3J 1P3

Voice: 416-736-2100 ext. 88828
Fax: 416-736-5686
E-mail: tklassen@yorku.ca

[I took two half-year courses from Prof. Klassen in 2004-05; one on public policy, the other on research methods]

Ms. Simone Wisdom
Manager, Customer Complaints
xxx
xxx
xxx

Voice:
Fax:
E-mail:

[Ms. Wisdom is my current employer]

Mr. Markut Smart
Coordinator
xxx
xxx
xxx

Voice:
Fax:
E-mail:

[Mr. Smart manages the community center where I have been volunteering for two years]

GENDER AND JOBS

One of the most important trends in the job market in recent years is the attempt on the part of large organizations and their human resources departments to eliminate gender discrimination in hiring and promotion. Despite the progress, however, it remains the case that:

- gender stereotypes are prevalent in the professional world;

- women are interviewed differently from men;

- significant prejudice exists with respect to interviews for the higher executive positions;

- promotions and raises are more difficult for women to achieve.

When it comes to interviewing, many women face a Catch-22. Successful interviewing means being assertive, but some employers - male and female – are threatened by women that appear aggressive. Success in the workplace is measured by continual upward mobility, but women are still expected to have children and raise them.

Getting a job depends on demonstrating one's skills, but many women have been brought up to downplay those skills in order to avoid appearing too masculine and competitive. Some conflict is expected when it comes to negotiating salary and promotion, but women are traditionally expected to diffuse conflict.

Many women need to take these stereotypes and attitudes into account because of the effect that they might have on the interview process and their progress on the job. Julie King[2] suggests that women need to pay particular attention to:

- building self-confidence prior to the interview;

- making the most of their superior listening and communication skills;

· defining and internalizing their personal accomplishments;

· taking greater charge of the interview process;

· anticipating, and preparing, for objections; and

· researching their professional and financial worth.

If the professional prospects for women in the past were limited, some characteristics of the modern workplace are more encouraging. In today's flatter and more dynamic organizations, communication, collaboration and consensus building are preferred to the more macho characteristics of entrepreneurial or hierarchical capitalism. The skills most commonly associated with women have become more important in professional settings.

AFTER THE INTERVIEW

Be aware that some employers try to keep candidates on the hook while they make a decision or negotiate with the leading candidate. While it's natural for them to look after their own self-interest, it's equally important for you to look after yours. If employers ask, as they often will, you can tell them that you are interviewing for other comparable positions. If they are reasonable, they will understand. If they are interested, it will make them act more quickly.

The wait after an interview can be lengthy and feel even lengthier. There is not much you can do, other than continue to look for jobs and go to interviews. Getting depressed will not help.

You are in the labor market and as in any market – whether the stock market, the pork bellies market, oil market or whatever – there has to be a match between the seller (you) and the buyer (the potential employers). This match will not occur immediately and likely not during the first attempt. Wait for a good match between your interests and abilities and the employment position.

Of course, counseling patience is easier than practicing it. But if you know that multiple opportunities typically result between 4 – 6 months of active networking and the job search, the tension should be manageable. Remember as well that you will probably get a job much closer to your own interests and aptitudes if you follow our advice.

As you wait for replies from employers, keep in touch with your network and keep looking for other employment positions. Things will work out!

NOTES

[1] Note that the percentages add up to more than 100% because many people use several strategies in their job search and because networking includes things like talking to professors and relatives.

[2] J.A. King (1995). *The smart woman's guide to interviewing and salary negotiation.* Franklin Lanes, NJ: Career Press.

CHAPTER EIGHT

HOW TO APPLY WHAT YOU LEARNED TO SUCCEED AT WORK

What is the recipe for successful achievement? To my mind there are just four essential ingredients: Choose a career you love, give it the best there is in you, seize your opportunities, and be a member of the team.

Benjamin F. Fairless

YOU'VE LANDED YOUR FIRST JOB AFTER GRADUATION. GREAT!

For a few weeks or months you will feel much like you did in your first year at university. It will be a time of transition and new expectations. You'll not know much and will need to figure things out quickly. Fortunately, your university years will have prepared you to absorb lots of information and make sense of it, and hopefully also provided you with the skills to make your own unique contribution.

At first you may be disappointed by your job. It may have sounded exciting in the interview, but now as you begin to learn what it is really all about, you begin to realize that you are starting at the bottom. Your customers, students, clients, shifts, projects and assignments are those that no one else wanted, the dregs.

And you know that's no accident. Just before you arrived on the scene others scooped up all the best assignments. But don't despair. You were hired exactly for the reason that there was no one available or willing to do these less appealing tasks. You've got your foot in the door. Now is the time to demonstrate that you can learn rapidly and contribute, while graciously accepting that you are the new kid on the block.

What your colleagues and superiors will be assessing now, more than at any future point in your career, is your personality. By showing that you are a contributor rather than a whiner at this difficult time, you can leave an indelible impression on others, one that will serve you well when opportunities arise for advancement in the future.

Often there comes a desire to move ahead too quickly. If you think that after two weeks you've discovered a great new way of doing things that has never been considered before, think again. It is highly unlikely that you have a solution to some longstanding problem after a few weeks on the job.

It is also insulting and irritating to your colleagues and superiors to assume that you know better than they do. You will get a reputation for being cocky and you certainly won't be looked upon as a team player. If only out of courtesy and respect, it is important to proceed cautiously at this stage.

At the same time, don't discount your observations either. By being new – and bringing to bear your university knowledge and expertise – you do, in fact, have a contribution to make. In fact, your newness is a real advantage because it allows you to look at patterns and processes with fresh eyes.

Keep a diary or notes during the first few weeks, because once you have been at an organization for a while you tend to accept things as they are or are becoming. Everyone has a natural tendency to slide into routine and become less able to question the taken-for-granted assumptions. You may feel that tendency all the more because you desperately want to establish a comfort zone for yourself in your new position.

If you eventually want to make a positive contribution – particularly by thinking critically or *outside of the box* – it is crucial that you strive to maintain that sense of newness, curiosity and questioning as long as possible. When you combine that fresh perspective with a bit more experience, you will add value to any organization.

As well, begin to specialize at work. Learn to do some tasks that others cannot do as well. These may even be some of the least interesting tasks that nobody else wants to do, but it is a very good idea to learn some of them because: 1) being able to do them well allows you to add immediate value; 2) there are few better ways to get to really understand a business or process than learning basic tasks; and 3) you are beginning to define the kind of person and employee that you will become.

One of the most frequently voiced complaints of corporate recruiters is that too many university graduates lack collaborative skills. Therefore, you can make a very good impression by demonstrating that you are a team player. If you learned how to work in groups at university, this will pay dividends for you now.

If you know yourself to be a good team player, you may have the tendency to want to immediately be included in projects. The danger here is that you will look too pushy and aggressive. Be patient. Your superiors and colleagues undoubtedly will *feel you out* as a person and assess your talents before including you. Don't worry; they'll discover your potential soon enough!

When this happens, you may find yourself besieged by requests for assistance. Large and complex organizations tend to divide work into projects and employees usually work on a number of projects simultaneously. This means that you may need to learn to play many different roles. Your experience role-playing in groups at university will help you here.

Also, you may have many different supervisors or colleagues depending on the number of projects in which you are involved. They may not be aware of all the work that you are doing. Even if they are, it is human nature for project managers to believe that their project is the only important one. So they will think that their timetable and deadline is the only one that counts!

Fortunately, you have lots of related experience dealing with university professors who all seem to set their assignment deadlines in the same week. You've learned a lot about managing your time and working backwards from deadlines. Hopefully, you've also learned that some tasks are more difficult, and some jobs and professors/employers are more demanding than others.

Trust yourself to make the necessary adjustments. Aim for competence and even excellence. But don't expect perfection. Nobody's perfect, but a lot of people have *burned themselves out* by trying to be!

As you learn on the job, use the same skills that you developed at university. Make a schedule for yourself just as you did at university. Prioritize your tasks; provide something extra in terms of the way you research and carry through projects. Use your critical skills to identify what is most essential. Above all else, demonstrate initiative and take any criticisms well. Your success at work will in large part be determined by how well you have used your time at university to learn, and hone, the skills that you need to be successful.

Instead of finding the first weeks or months at your job stressful or an adjustment you might just find them fun-filled and exciting. Hey, you're making money; you don't have term papers and essays to worry about. You may have your weekends free to enjoy yourself and your hobbies (although many jobs in today's workforce extend the working week). As well, you're meeting new people, learning and being provided with the opportunity to demonstrate some new skills and abilities.

It does occasionally happen that something like this initial excitement continues all the way through your career. However, it's common for this initial enthusiasm to wear off. After a few months or a year at work, a lot of people get a little depressed. You're still in the same chair, in the same cubicle, doing the same tasks. Your work may not be fulfilling and you're not sure even if it is being recognized. The daily grind of routine sets in with a break of only two weeks, instead of four months, on your mental horizon. Your initial excitement begins to dissipate and you're dying for a change. Any change!

These feelings are natural. Unlike university, managers rarely dole out grades or comments. There are few transcripts that summarize what you have learned or accomplished (job evaluations may take place only once a year). Instead of working with several teachers and many different colleagues, you will typically have a smaller social group to stimulate you.

Then there's the hierarchy that characterizes corporations and larger organizations. It may seem that you are at the bottom of a very long ladder. Everyone else is above you and they appear to be constantly watching your behavior. Sure, at university, your professors had some power over you. But that power was limited to one course that you could always drop if you had to. And, for every bad professor or TA, there likely was a good one who challenged or stimulated you.

Ironically, after four years dreaming about graduating and getting out, you might actually find yourself missing being a student. At least at university there was something to look forward to. At least once a year, you got to experience new classes, new classmates, new professors, and new books. Plus, it's hard to beat several weeks' vacation, not counting the summer holidays.

If this happens, remember that things are not as bad as they look. It may take a year or even two in order to get accustomed to the new rhythms of the workplace. But, gradually you will find that the rewards of a challenging and fulfilling job more than compensate for a student's life. The feeling you get, not only from mastering tasks, but also applying them in the real world, is a very satisfying one. Moreover, you can always use those critical and creative skills to make your projects more gratifying.

If you find that you miss university, you can always return to take a course. Many employers will even pay part or all of your tuition, if you demonstrate that the course you wish to complete is related to your employment position. But why not take a course in something that has nothing to do with your job – on a subject that interests you? That's one of the best ways to keep the creative juices flowing.

Also, consider what is essential about what you are missing. If it is change that you are missing, try to find ways to vary your job. If it is self-development, use your now free evenings and weekends to explore interests that you never had time for before. If you want to develop more in-depth skills or insights, be proactive in looking for opportunities to do this in your new profession. You've become an expert at learning, so begin to motivate and teach yourself inside and outside your job.

Most of all, don't limit your options. A broadly based university education, and particularly a liberal arts education, provides you with something that you just can't get from any form of specialized or professional training – adaptability. Your ability to adapt is what every employer is looking for, but you can also make it work for you.

MANY OPTIONS

The ultimate advantage that your university degree gives you, with regard to the job market, is flexibility. In Ontario, 96% of all university graduates are employed within six months of graduation, with 81% of them employed in positions that were "closely" or "somewhat closely" related to their university education.[1]

The very low unemployment rates of university students, combined with relatively high incomes[2], mean unparalleled options to pursue different careers: self-employment, volunteer work, full and part-time work, permanent and contract work, jobs in other countries, and so many more.

One of the reasons that it is so difficult to talk to students about *what the hell is a university degree good for* is that it's good for so many things. You'll find university graduates in all sorts of positions that appear to have little relationship to their university major or field of studies.

What's equally fascinating is how well university graduates do in so many different fields. They pull in roughly the same income as those who specialize in technical or administrative areas at colleges or vocational institutes, but they move more freely around in a much wider and more exciting world. The skills that they've developed not only make them indispensable to their employers and allow them to move up the ladder reasonably quickly. But university graduates also have unparalleled freedom to change jobs and even start up their own businesses.

This flexibility is demonstrably true for men, but even more the case for women. A woman's average income, level of responsibility, and employment options increase significantly when she has a university degree. Even though the notorious *glass ceiling* does get in the way of women's advancement, a university degree remains the best investment any woman could ever make.

DEALING WITH THE TRANSITION

The transition from school to university is not always a smooth one. But university, despite all its stresses, is an environment that can become too comfortable for some students. By the time you graduate you will have pretty well figured out how things work. And, if you learn to be a good student, you are not just comfortable but you are probably having a great deal of fun.

In university, the timeframe that you tend to work within is a few months, from the beginning to the end of the semester. You advance in regular steps and get a degree within a relatively short period of time. At work, your career trajectory becomes considerably elastic, with significant changes often taking much longer than you might expect.

It is an axiom that today's workplace is characterized by change. But, that does not necessarily apply to your personal advancement. In fact, your parents probably had opportunities for much more rapid promotion because, as baby boomers, they moved into the positions left vacant by the death or retirement of a more equally distributed demographic cohort. But, many of today's best jobs are hogged by the people from your parent's generation.

Don't be too impatient. You will find your own comfort zone in the workplace eventually. The baby boomers are rapidly approaching retirement age and you can look forward to considerably more opportunities for advancement in just a few years. If you are just starting university now, your future prospects are particularly good.

If you are really unhappy or impatient in your position, it probably means that this is not the right job for you and you need to make additional changes in your life. Don't look upon those employment changes as a bad thing to be feared. Consider them an opportunity for growth and renewed excitement.

After a while

After a few months or a year you may decide that your job is not as great as you thought it would be. That's perfectly normal. After all, it is unlikely that your very first job after graduation will be your ideal one for the rest of your life. Most graduates have two jobs during their first two years after graduation. The strategies and suggestions in this book can help as you search for that perfect fit between who you are and the requirements of a position.

The advice we gave you about choosing your university courses is exactly the same for deciding on a job. Follow what feels right. Consult your interests, your desires, and your dreams. Below we briefly discuss the strategies that any professional, at any stage of his or her career, needs to follow.

Keep your resume up-to-date

Your resume becomes more important than ever after you have started to work full-time. Revise it every few months as you undertake new tasks and learn new skills. If you're continuing your education on a part-time basis, be sure to indicate this. You will be surprised how often, at short notice, you will be asked for your resume.

In addition to keeping your resume current, you will need to keep your list of references current as well. Your employer will be your key reference. Don't burn bridges, even if that means biting your tongue and swallowing your pride — hard, at times, to be sure. But, years later, you'll be glad you did it and you may even look upon difficult employers with greater fondness.

Once you've decided that you want to move on, you once again need to do research. You will have developed your network while working and can start to touch base with key contacts. It is best to look for a job while still employed, so leaving is usually not recommended until you have a firm offer.

Of course, that depends on the job you have. Some jobs are so demanding in terms of time or pressure that you simply don't have the leisure to think, let alone engage in a job search. Some jobs don't provide you with the kind of contacts you need to build a decent network. Such jobs tend to be career dead ends. Bite the bullet; get out and begin a new job search.

If you do leave a position without a new one in hand, you need to make sure that you maintain your confidence. This is particularly true because it is likely to take you several months of hard work to find a good job. When you doubt yourself, it's a good idea to reflect on what you achieved by completing a university degree. If you could do that, you can do anything.

A second piece of advice is to avoid brooding about your situation. You won't feel unemployed if you treat your job search as a full time job. Get up early each day; dress as though you were going to work; build up your network; go for informational interviews; rethink your career path and assess your options. Looking for a job is the hardest job you will ever have. If you do it well, you won't have time to get depressed and you'll eventually be successful.

One key ingredient for success that we've spoken about too little in this book is confidence. The success you've achieved at school gives you one kind of confidence; being successful at work gives you another. It is natural for any of us to lose a little of our self-confidence when we are not being successful in our work.

Being unemployed and looking for work tends to have a negative impact on our confidence, which is why we recommend looking for a new job while still being employed. But if you find yourself unemployed at some point in your career, you can always draw on one special kind of emotional currency — the self-esteem that comes from completing a university degree and doing well in your courses.

You can also use your research and reading skills to help you cope with negative periods in your life and to develop the personal skills that will increase your chances of success. Although the world we live in contains a lot of anxiety and depression, there is an abundant literature available on how to become a happier, more confident person. The authors highly recommend David Burns *The Feeling Good Handbook*[3] as a starting place.

LEARNING DOES NOT END WITH A JOB

Be aware that your learning will not end once you start work. Just consider that those people in senior professional positions today were taught how to use slide rulers in primary and secondary school. These individuals were never exposed to computers until well into their careers. Think of the learning they had to do. You will be faced with similar challenges as technology, laws and professional standards change during your career.

The rate of change is increasing dramatically as we are moving into the twenty-first century. Fluidity and flexibility have now become bywords in the global marketplace. In a world characterized by constant change, the kind of skill set developed at university is much more relevant than it ever has been in the past. But it is up to you – not your parents, your professors, or your employers – to make it alive and relevant in the present.

GRADUATE, PROFESSIONAL AND VOCATIONAL SCHOOLS

After some time in the labor force your thoughts might turn to further education. It is very likely that you will know better what your ideal job truly is after a year or more at work. Many professional and graduate schools look highly upon applicants who have experience in the labor force. Be sure to use that experience to your advantage.

Graduate and professional schools are most concerned about accepting applicants who will complete the program and then contribute to the profession. Applying for graduate and professional school is similar to applying for jobs. The one thing that all graduate and professional programs want to avoid at all costs is students who will become problems because they do not fit, cannot follow the rules, and so forth.

We are often asked by professional schools to provide references for students that we have taught. Their overriding question and concern is not how smart or academically promising the candidate is. It is whether the student has *what it takes* to successfully complete the program and whether or not this is the kind of person who will eventually become a good colleague in their profession.

In your application materials, demonstrate that you have carefully considered how you can, and desire, to make a contribution to your desired profession. Use your network to provide the kind of references that support your statements. Be tenacious, even if you don't succeed the first time around, or look for different avenues to your goal such as part-time study. It is rare that there is only one route to your destination.

If your grades were not particularly high when you were an undergraduate student, be sure to explain why this was the case. Then demonstrate that your capacity to learn, as well as your motivation, has increased since your undergraduate days. A few good grades in part-time courses will probably convince them that you now have what it takes.

Volunteer work will also help to show that your academic transcript fails to fully reflect your skills and abilities. In some professions, such as education and business, these volunteer activities are weighted almost as heavily as your academic scores.

Some graduate and professional programs require writing standardized exams, such as the LSAT, GMAT, etc. The key to acing these exams is practicing the types of questions they ask. There are a number of books available that contain sample questions and strategies. Those who work through them score significantly higher than those who don't.

Finally, you will need letters of reference for your application, some of which will need to be from professors. Here you will have been wise and kept in touch with a professor or two. As well, if you've kept copies of your assignments that you can offer as a reminder of the quality of work you produced in past courses, you will be guaranteed a strong letter of reference.

Avoid asking for a letter of reference a few days before it is due. Rather, ask in person and give your referee several weeks if possible. This way you can renew your acquaintance, make sure the professor remembers you, and give him or her a copy of your resume to show what you have done since graduation.

Always ask for a copy of your referee's letter. Some potential referees will object that letters of reference are supposed to be confidential. That probably means that they are not going to compose a very strong letter for you. Even if you think otherwise, you simply cannot afford to take such a risk. It is your future; you need to know exactly what is being said about you. Go ask someone else if a potential referee is not forthcoming.

Applying for graduate or professional school is a considerable amount of work, and entails much research. The deadlines for applications are sometimes almost a year in advance of the start of the program. You need to have a clear idea of the kind of research or program that you want to pursue. A hurried application, like a sloppy resume, is a waste of time. Trust us on this one; we have a lot of experience.

Community college education

For some university graduates a community college diploma or certificate is the best complement to achieving success in the workplace. In fact, the combination of university and college courses is becoming common.

Again, there is research involved, including discussion with your network about whether this option is best for you. Generally, a community college diploma is a good route if you have little work experience and/or you know exactly the type of job that you wish to obtain.

MENTORING AND NETWORKING

As you advance your career you will continue to require the support of your network and must actively keep it operational. The term used by career advisors is *keeping your network warm*. For some individuals this becomes second nature, while for some this is a task that must be scheduled and planned for.

Remember that a network works both ways. Now you may have university students coming and asking you for informational interviews. Treat them as you would have wished to be treated when you were conducting your interviews. Remember that what goes around, comes around. These students will help keep your network *warm* as they make contact with the people you recommend to them.

FURTHER SUCCESS

The road to the great job is just that, a road. You may reach your ideal job, only to discover that it is less so. Life simply is sometimes like that. The words of those aging rockers, the Rolling Stones, should be taken to heart: "You can't always get what you want." "But, if you try sometimes, you just might find…you get what you need."

You will encounter difficulties on the road, some possibly based on your gender, ethnic background or personality. Again, the key is to trust your feelings and nourish your dreams. If a work situation or experience does not feel right, it is likely that there is a poor match between your expertise and interests, and the requirements of the position.

As you progress in the world of work, you will gain more experience (especially in trusting your feelings!) and acquire colleagues and associates who you can trust and from whom you can get advice. The support of your network will be critical to your success and happiness. One or more of your professors may well be a part of the support and networking group. More than likely some of the friends from your university days will be as well.

Sometimes the mentor needs mentoring

Many university professors, because they are very busy and have research and administrative commitments, don't keep in touch with students who could help other students succeed in the job market. They occasionally need to be reminded that they have taught many students who now work in many different fields and with whom they still have influence. When you become established in your chosen career, visit your old professor and department. Offer to give a talk or seminar to students on job prospects. You'll be doing everyone a big favor.

Regardless of your path, you have all the advantages that you acquired at university: problem solving, good communication skills, strategic and creative thinking, adaptability and the self-confidence that accomplishing a university degree brings. Use these well and your success is assured.

Finally, remember that, at the end of the day, success isn't only about job security, money or social recognition. It is all about flourishing. Don't just work at your job. Work also at being happy and *flourishing* in whatever career or careers you choose.

NOTES

[1] Ontario University Graduate Survey: www.ouac.on.ca/news/2000_survey.pdf.

[2] The 2001 Census found that Canadians with a university degree earn $20,000 more a year than those without a university degree.

[3] Burns, David D. (1999). *The feeling good handbook*. New York: Penguin Putman Inc.

SOURCES

GENERAL SOURCES

Bates, A. W. (1999). *Managing technological change: Strategies for college and university leaders.* San Francisco: Jossey-Bass.

Beatty, R. H. (1977). *The perfect cover letter.* New York: John Wiley.

Bloom, B.S. (ed) *Taxonomy of Educational Objectives: Vol. I: Cognitive Domain* (New York: McKay, 1956).

Bolles, R. N. (2005). *What color is your parachute?: A practical manual for job hunters and career changers.* Berkeley, CA: Ten Speed Press.

Burns, David D. (1999). *The feeling good handbook.* New York: Penguin Putman Inc.

Cameron, J. with Bryan, M. (1992). *The artist's way: A spiritual path to higher creativity.* New York: G.P. Putnam.

French, J. N. and Rhoder, C. (1992). *Teaching thinking skills: Theory and practice.* New York: Garland Publishing.

Gebremedhin, T. G. and Tweeten, L.G. (1994). *Research methods and communication in the social sciences.* Westport, CT: Praeger.

Gilbert, M. (1996). *How to win an argument.* New York: John Wiley.

Herr, E. L., and Cramer, S.H. (1992). *Career guidance and counseling through the lifespan.* New York: Harper Collins.

Jarvis, P. (2003). *Career Management Paradigm Shift.* Ottawa: National Life/Work Centre. www.contactpoint.ca/resources/dbase.php?type=user_query&fetchid=1469

King, J. A. (1995). *The smart woman's guide to interviewing and salary negotiation.* Franklin Lanes, NJ: Career Press.

Klassen, T. R. and Dwyer, J. (2003). *A practical guide to getting a great job after university: Or how to flourish in both university and the labour market.* Toronto: York University.

Norman, D. A. (1994). *Things that make us smart: Defending human attributes in the age of the machine.* Don Mills, ON: Addison-Wesley.

Powers, P. (2005). *Winning job interviews.* Franklin Lakes, NJ: Career Press.

Whetten, D. A. and Cameron, K. S. (1998). *Developing management skills.* Don Mills, ON.: Addison-Wesley.

Yate, M. (2004). *Resumes that knock 'em dead.* Avon, MA: Adams Media Corporation.

OTHER HELPFUL RESOURCES

1. Critical Skills

Chang, R. Y. and Kelly, P. K. (1996) *Step-by-step problem solving.* Irvine, CA: Richard Chang Associates.

Crux, S. C. (1991). *Learning strategies for adults: Compensations for learning disabilities.* Toronto: Wall and Emerson.

Dwyer, J. A. (2003). *Learning to listen actively.* Unpublished manuscript. Available from the author upon request. Send requests to jdwyer@yorku.ca.

Dwyer, J. A. (2003). *Reading actively.* Unpublished manuscript. Available from the author upon request. Send requests to jdwyer@yorku.ca.

Dwyer, J. A. (2003). *Researching your topic.* Unpublished manuscript. Available from the author upon request. Send requests to jdwyer@yorku.ca.

Fleet, J., Goodchild, F. and Zajchowski, R. (1994). *Learning for success: Skills and strategies for Canadian students.* Toronto: Harcourt Brace.

McWhorter, K. T. (1986). *College reading and study skills.* Boston: Little, Brown.

Pauk, W. (1993). *How to study in college.* Boston: Houghton-Mifflin.

Robinson, F. P. (1961). *Effective study.* New York: Harper & Row.

Ruggerio, V. R. (1996). *Becoming a critical thinker.* Boston: Houghton-Mifflin

Shea, V. and Whitla, W. (2001). *Foundations: Critical thinking, reading and writing.* Toronto: Pearson.

2. Writing

Academic Skill Centre, Trent University (1995). *Thinking it through: A practical guide to academic essay writing.* Peterborough, ON: Trent University.

Bly, R. W. (1999). *The encyclopedia of business letters, fax memos, and e-mail.* Franklin Lakes, NJ: Career Press.

Cioffi, F. L. (2005). *The imaginative argument: A practical manifesto for writers.* Princeton, Princeton University Press.

Cooley, M. E. (1993). *The inventive writer: Using critical thinking to persuade.* Lexington, Mass.: D.C. Heath.

Dwyer, J. A. (2003). *The art of note taking.* Unpublished manuscript. Available from the author upon request. Send requests to jdwyer@yorku.ca.

Dwyer, J. A. (2003). *Composing a case study.* Unpublished manuscript. Available from the author upon request. Send requests to jdwyer@yorku.ca.

Fry, E. and Sakiey, E. (1997). *Writer's manual.* Chicago: Contemporary Books.

Gaidosch, B. (1994). *Common sense: A short guide to essay writing.* Toronto: Harcourt Brace.

Germano, W. (2005). *From dissertation to book.* Chicago: University of Chicago Press.

Green, B. and Norton, S. (1995). *Essay essentials.* Toronto: Harcourt Brace.

Kiniry, M. and Rose, M. (1993). *Critical strategies for academic thinking and writing. A text and reader.* Boston: Bedford Books.

Lispon, C. (2004). *Doing honest work in college: How to prepare citations, avoid plagiarism, and achieve real academic success.* Chicago: Chicago Guides to Writing, Editing, and Publishing.

Nothey, M. and McKibbion, J. (2005). *Making sense: A student's guide to research and writing.* Canada: Oxford University Press.

Power, B. M. (1996). *Taking note: Improving your observational notetaking.* York, ME: Stenhouse Publishers.

Robinson, F. P. (1962). *Effective reading.* New York: Harper & Row.

Ross-Larson, B. (2002). *Writing for the information age.* New York: W.W. Norton & Company.

Sawers, N. (2000). *Ten steps to help you write better essays and term papers.* Edmonton: The NS Group.

Strath, L., Avery, H. and Taylor, K. (1993). *Notes on the preparation of essays in the arts and sciences.* Peterborough: ON: Trent University Academic Skills Centre.

Strunk, W. and White, E. B. (2000). *The elements of style.* New York: Longman.

Turabian, K. L. (1996). *A manual for writers of term papers, theses, and dissertations.* Chicago: University of Chicago Press.

Walliman, N. (2004). *Your undergraduate dissertation: The essential guide for success.* Thousand Oaks: Sage Publications.

3. Presentations

Berg, K. and Gilman, A. (1989). *Get to the point.* New York: Bantam Books.

Campbell, D. (1974). *If you don't know where you're going, you'll probably end up somewhere else.* Niles, IL: Argus Communications.

Cole, M. And Odenwald, S. (1990). *Desktop presentations.* New York: AMACOM Books.

Harvard University Business School. (2004). *Presentations that persuade and motivate.* Boston: Harvard Business School Press.

Mandel, S. (1998). *Technical presentation skills.* Los Altos, CA: Crisp Publications.

Rafe, S. C. (1990). *How to be prepared to think on your feet.* New York: Harper Business.

Runion, M. (2004) *How to use power phrases to say what you mean, mean what you say, and get what you want.* New York: McGraw-Hill.

Tufte, E. R (1983). *The visual display of quantitative information.* Cheshire, CT.: Graphics Press.

Westerfield, J. (2002). *I have to give a presentation, now what?!* New York: Silver Lining Books

4. Useful Study and Exam Skills Links

Charles Sturt University:
www.hsc.csu.edu.au/study/links.htm

UK university site:
http://web.apu.ac.uk/stu_services/essex/learningsupport/LSwebistes02.htm

University of Western Ontario's Student Development Centre:
www.sdc.uwo.ca/learning

York University Learning Skills Program:
www.yorku.ca/cdc/lsp/index.htm

York University Faculty of Arts Writing Centre:
http://www.arts.yorku.ca/caw/

5. The Best Canadian Career Sites

A career tool with information on hundreds of occupational groups
and work experiences of recent graduates: www.jobfutures.ca/en/home.shtml

Current trends and future outlook for occupations in Ontario:
www1.on.hrdc-drhc.gc.ca/ojf/ojf.jsp

A review of wages paid to workers in more than 200 different occupations
in Ontario: www.onestep.on.ca/ows/Ows99_Eng/welcome_e.html

For those interested in working in the non-profit sector: www.charityvillage.com

York University Career Centre: www.yorku.ca/careers

6. Canadian web sites with job listings:

www.jobsetc.ca

www.working.canada.com/index_map.html

www.gojobs.gov.on.ca/mbs/gojobs/gojobs.nsf/GOjobsHome

See also the York University Career Center:
www.yorku.ca/careers and www.yorku.ca/careers/cyberguide

The authors would be pleased to provide an electronic version of these links. Please e-mail either John Dwyer at jdwyer@yorku.ca or Thomas Klassen at tklassen@yorku.ca

AUTHORS

John A. Dwyer is a Professor in the Business and Society Program in the Division of Social Science at York University. He currently teaches the second year Foundations course in Business and Society as well as a graduate course on the eighteenth-century Enlightenment.

By training as an historian of ideas and culture, Professor Dwyer has written and/or edited four books on eighteenth-century life and culture. He has also written a textbook used by business schools entitled Business History: Canada in the Global Community. He has a particular interest in the philosopher and economist, Adam Smith.

John Dwyer worked for many years as a teacher, administrator and consultant. He has held a number of different positions, including Acting Placement Director for the Schulich School of Business, where he liaised with employers and helped broker matches between graduates and companies. He has also worked as a frontier educator, a university fundraiser, a professional career developer, as the Associate Director of a university teaching center, and as President of his own business, Ivory Tower Communications, where he provided consulting services to universities and colleges.

Professor Dwyer can be reached at: jdwyer@yorku.ca

Thomas R. Klassen is an Associate Professor in the Department of Political Science at York University, and Coordinator of the Public Policy and Administration Program. He teaches courses on Canadian politics and public administration.

Professor Klassen is the author of *Precarious Values: Organizations, Politics and Labor Market Policy in Ontario* and numerous academic and policy articles on the nature of work and the labor market. As a person who stutters, he also conducts research on the experience of persons with disabilities.

He has presented papers at conferences in Europe, Africa and North America. His writings have also appeared in the Toronto Star, the Globe and Mail and other publications. Dr. Klassen has been a consultant on workplace and labor market issues to community agencies, legal firms, and the Ontario and federal governments.

Prior to becoming a professor, he worked for ten years as a policy advisor at Queen's Park in both social and economic policy.

Professor Klassen can be reached at: tklassen@yorku.ca or via his web site: www.arts.yorku.ca/politics/tklassen